HACKNEY LIBRARY SERVICES

May 2007

150
67
13
99
638

WITHDRAWN

D0997129

The Old Bird remembers…

incorporating

Margaret's Story

Portrait of John in the late 1960s

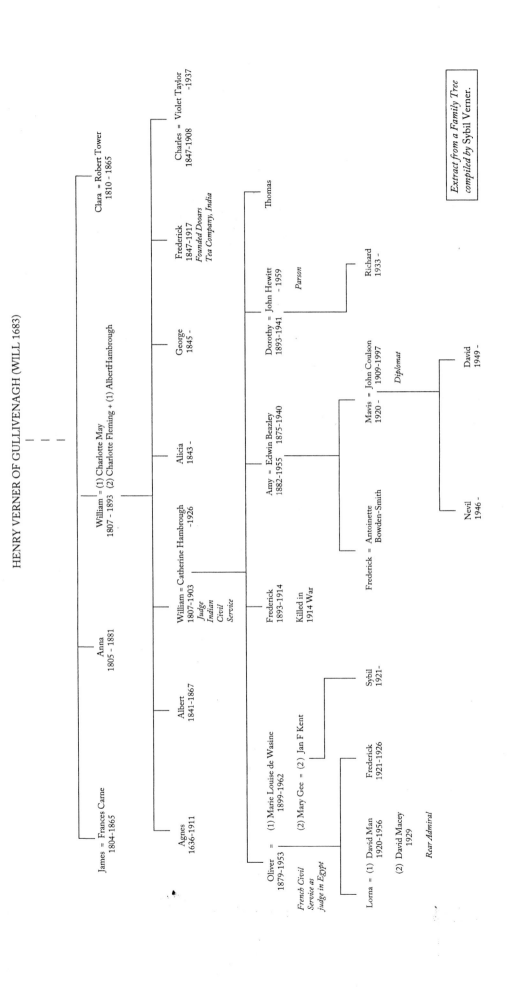

HENRY VERNER OF GULLIVENAGH (WILL 1683)

James = Frances Carne
1804-1865

Anna
1805 - 1881

William = (1) Charlotte May
1807 - 1893   (2) Charlotte Fleming + (1) Albert Hambrough

Clara = Robert Tower
1810 - 1865

Agnes
1636-1911

Albert
1841-1867

William = Catherine Hambrough
1807-1903   -1926
Judge Indian Civil Service

Alicia
1843 -

George
1845 -

Frederick
1847-1917
Founded Dooars Tea Company, India

Charles = Violet Taylor
1847-1908   -1937

Oliver =
1879-1953
French Civil Service as judge in Egypt

(1) Marie Louise de Wasine
1899-1962

(2) Mary Gee = (2) Jan F Kent

Sybil
1921-

Frederick
1893-1914
Killed in 1914 War

Amy = Edwin Beazley
1882-1955   1875-1940

Dorothy = John Hewitt
1893-1941   -1959
Parson

Thomas

Richard
1933 -

Lorna = (1) David Man
1920-1956

(2) David Macey
1929
Rear Admiral

Frederick
1921-1926

Frederick = Antoinette
Bowden-Smith

Mavis = John Coulson
1920 -   1909-1997
Diplomat

Nevil
1946 -

David
1949 -

Extract from a Family Tree compiled by Sybil Verner.

ACKNOWLEDGEMENTS

"This book might not have 'happened' without the support and encouragement of my two sons, Nevil and David. The early drafts were typed by Olivia Thompson, as were the captions just before going to press. Nevil and David helped edit the different drafts, as did other friends such as Alistair Langlands. My nephew, Andrew Beazley helped enormously by finding and scanning many old family photos for me from Freddy's albums. The early contemporary photos in the book were taken by John and me and by friends and many of the later photos were taken by my photographer son, David. The portrait of me (on the last page) was taken recently by Angela Fisher. David found, digitised and captioned 150 images with the invaluable help of his Nairobi staff, in particular Nina White and Judy Payne. I have been greatly helped in launching this book by Chawton House Library (where I was for a while 'writer in residence') and Susie Grandfield, who has been invaluable in organising the event in conjunction with Olivia. Lastly, the title was the idea of Damon de Laszlo. Perhaps most of all I would like to say thank you to my friend, Barney Wan, ably assisted by Rob Skipper, who has done such a wonderful job of designing this book."

The Old Bird remembers...

CONTENTS

CHAPTER ONE – *Unexpected Communication*

"Ottawa Canada" 1980

Dear Mavis,

As you remember, when I was in hospital I gave you my dagger for keeping and now will you please, to be so kind and send me it back. I am sorry to ask you for that, but for you this dagger have no special value and I want to give it to the museum in Ottawa where will be open a special section for Polish military memorabilia, to commemorate our participation in the last war."

This somewhat unexpected missive reached me one morning thirty-five years after I had known the sender. By a series of coincidences, it found me quite quickly – as no doubt Sq. Leader Krasnodemski was certain it would do. All the same, I sat and marvelled at the confidence with which he had written. Thirty-five years is (soberingly) thirty-five years and, since I had married we had lived in a variety of countries – under at least twenty different roofs.

And the dagger…Yes, the dagger had accompanied us to many places. The prized possession of our younger son, it had hung for years on his bedroom wall.

I had often wondered what had become of Sq. Leader Krasnodemski. As I read his letter the whole thing now came back to me – East Grinstead Hospital, only five miles from Parrock Wood, our home. It was here that I was reunited with Anne Bowden-Smith who was later to become my sister-in-law. She and I had met at Red Cross lectures after leaving school three months earlier. I vividly remember a brilliant September day in 1941 when we rode horses and picnicked in nearby woods, watching the planes above us through the birch-lace in one of the earliest dogfights of what became known as the "Battle of Britain". Now I found myself a giggling ingenue in Red Cross Uniform, reporting for duty to Archie McIndoe's 3rd Degree Burn Ward; Ward Two for men and Ward Three for women. They were organised respectively by Sisters Mealy and Harrington – two Irish Sisters of a breed unknown today. Sister Mealy was tiny and would have slipped through the proverbial keyhole with ease.

Her minute waist was encased in the traditional dark blue petersham which exuded authority and from the beginning she eyed me with contempt. Sister Harrington directed

Ward Two, where Anne was posted. She was the opposite to Sister Mealy, a pretty Irish redhead who, to our great approval, was having a discreet affair with our house surgeon.

Poor sister Mealy; I must have been anathema to her! This little Irishwoman (old to me but certainly not a day over 28) was the soul of discipline and order. In the autumn of 1940 the hospital had already expanded from Cottage Hospital to War Casualty Unit (with special emphasis on plastic surgery). Sir Archibald McIndoe had his own, now immortalised, theatre Staff and Sisters and there was, by today's standards, a high level of nursing. But the wards were full and steadily getting fuller. Battle of Britain heroes, victims of the Blitz, and so on, poured in. Help was urgently needed and, gradually, more and more V.A.D.s (Voluntary Aid Detachments) were brought in from local Red Cross Detachments. Most of us were housed in the Nurses' Home but, as I lived within easy 'bus distance, I used to come daily.

From early on I must have been the ward buffoon. Apochryphal, (and not so apocryphal either) stories seemed to attach themselves to me – a particular favourite concerning the day the Great Man came round the ward with the usual retinue of 40 odd students. Stopping to examine some unfortunate man with a sausage of skin-graft round his throat, he is said to have looked round, spotted an unfortunate V.A.D tidying a nearby locker, and called in stentorian tones: "Fetch me a brush, Nurse, quickly!" Legend has it that the V.A.D. leapt in the air, tore to the end of the ward where the cleaning staff kept their tools and came flying back with a floor broom. (Not me, I assure you…on that occasion.)

I have often wondered about the way we lived through that time. To say one enjoyed most parts of the war is no exaggeration. We were young, as yet unattached, we lived for the day and it never entered your head that anything could happen to us or to those who belonged to us. (Indeed, the idea of Britain not winning the war certainly never occurred to us). Above all, there was this tremendous feeling of stimulation everywhere – something, of course, we have been chasing ever since.

The Battle of Britain raged all round us when I first went to East Grinstead. Doctors and nurses in white and blue uniforms would slip out at moments to follow the head-on dog fights above. Unaware that History was being played out before our eyes, we watched this astonishing spectacle, which somehow bore no real relation to life and death. Happily counting the spiralling descending enemy planes, we cheered ourselves hoarse at the Galahad thrusts of our fighter-pilots – only stopping briefly to shudder as, once in a while, the enemy shot at a parachuting British airman…(It has become increasingly fashionable to deride our Battle of Britain as Old Sentimental Hat. One inevitably wonders whether this does not, in part at any rate, stem from a longing for some clear-cut issue of this kind in a world where sadly pride and good faith are often treated as dirty words.

For an ingenue – and I was one par excellence – Ward III at E. Grinstead was not easy on the susceptibilities. Here were gathered the worst victims of Trial by Fire – and, slowly, with infinitesimal care, Archie McIndoe put them together again. Richard Hillary, in "The Last Enemy", Tom Gleave in "I had a Row with a German", and Geoffrey Page have left first-hand and poignant accounts of this process. Archie was literally a saviour to these patients, and the way in which he built each one up, psychologically – to face what in the end could turn out to be least fifteen operations – was beyond praise.

Yes, psychology was the priority on Ward III. One walked a tight-rope where reactions to major disfigurement were concerned. A large proportion of the men were horribly burnt in the face – and, during the first stages of skin-graft operations, were not pleasant to look at. Between operations, these patients were allowed out in the town of East Grinstead, and it was some time before the 'locals' learned how to react to their appearance. Archie McIndoe would visit high street stores and talk with the young teenage shop assistants. On the ward you quickly understood that not only was any kind of pity ruled out, but revulsion, too. Nor was it acceptable to pretend to ignore a man's often hideous appearance. To get it right, in fact, was far from easy, and the sensitive were apt to find themselves becoming too hard, in self-protection.

On such a Ward, as I have already said, morale came before everything, and what was in those days the normal routine of strict discipline for nurses and visitors was waived. None of us who were associated with Ward III will ever forget the weekends, when Archie McIndoe regularly brought down his "Show Business" friends to cheer up the patients. (I wonder whether anyone has properly done justice to Ben Lyons, Bebe Daniels, and Frances Day (to name only a few) who used to give their scant free time to 'chatting up' a collection of men who would have done justice to Hieronymus Bosch at his worst. Sitting on the narrow iron ward beds, they revived a self-respect and will-to-live in countless men who might otherwise have given up. Not unnaturally the girls were best at this, and I remember particularly what Frances Day did for one young Pilot Officer of 19.

Peter Weekes had been as nearly burnt to pieces as makes no odds. He was conveyed with difficulty to East Grinstead and, once there, became the recipient of non-stop, intensive 3rd degree burn care (saline baths, tullegras and so on). Very gradually he began to improve -until the day his 16-year-old fiancée came to see him. This young girl, being clearly without preparation of any sort for life, wept hysterically when she saw him and broke off the engagement. Whereupon, Peter turned his face to the wall and proceeded to die slowly.

Some weeks later Frances Day came down to Ward III and Archie McIndoe asked whether she would pay particular attention to Peter (isolated, by then, in his own cubicle). Peter ignored her when she began 'chatting him up'. On the contrary, he kept his face averted and there appeared to be no contact. Suddenly she said: "Peter, my new Show is coming off in the West End in November." (This was August.) "I've got a brand-new song called: 'He wore a pair of Silver Wings', and it's going to be a knock-out. Peter…! You are going to be there for our First Night. Oh I don't care how you get there – but you'll be there. And I shall sing that song for you! Now remember, Peter, you'll be there. I'm counting on you."

Well, you've guessed it. From that moment on Peter began to improve. November 15th came and he was taken by ambulance to London, where a fire engine conveyed him to the theatre. While she sang the song, Peter was caught in a spotlight…He never looked back after that and, many years later, some time in the 70s, I found myself, by complete chance, sitting next to him at a buffet lunch given by my sister-in-law in Reigate. The emaciated, "already-in-the-other-world" Peter was now a solid, obviously successful member of society – headmaster, in fact, of a flourishing prep school in Hindhead – with a charming wife and a position in the educational world.

What, one asks oneself, is the in-built mechanism which makes us reject, in memory, the horrible, the unsatisfactory and, above all, the dreary? Looking back on those East Grinstead days, I seem for the most part to recall only the positive, the absurd, the shocking. I remember particularly the day they brought in two German airmen to Ward III. They had been shot down between East Grinstead and London and were not so much burnt as severely mutilated. Both of them were very young. Both of them kept up a non-stop stream of abuse as doctors and nurses attended them. We were endlessly reminded that Hitler was on the point of launching a major invasion of England – that we should be made to pay for it – and much more. One of them was nearly out of his mind, I remember, at having lost his Iron Cross. Feelings of compassion were soon stifled, however, when he spat at a passing nurse. I remember well our gentle efficient house surgeon struggling to save the life of a young pilot who never ceased to obstruct and curse him to the point when the surgeon laid down his instruments, saying quietly, "If you say another word I will leave you to die."

Half a century later, when the Germans are our brothers in Europe and we are allied together against the common enemies of Terrorism and Economic Disaster, one looks back in wonder at such incidents. Fortunately – oh! fortunately indeed – tout passe.

"Nurse, you're wanted in Sister's office." It was Monday morning and I had just come on duty from home, five miles away. Shivering, I tapped on her door, wondering what lapse I was about to be accused of. Could it be anything to do with the man I'd left too long in the bath yesterday – out of consideration for his modesty? Sister Mealy seemed distinctly excited. "Nurse, they tell me you speak French?" This was unexpected. "Ye-es, sister, – of a sort!" "Good. I want you to 'special' our new patient, then. He is a distinguished Polish officer, badly burned. He is Colonel Krasnodemski, Squadron Leader of General Sikorski's squadron 303. He arrived last night. We find it difficult to speak to him. You will concentrate on teaching him English as soon as you can. " She eyed me with her usual contempt as she drew herself up to her full, diminutive height (making me feel like an untethered hollyhock) and said crisply: "That'll be all, Nurse. No need to hang about. "

Five minutes later I was at my patient's bedside – trying to light a cigarette for him. Squadron Leader Krasnodemski, I had meanwhile learned, on hastily consulting the Ward grapevine, was something of an ace. It appeared he had been shot down in flames, while leading General Sikorski's famous Squadron 303 and, after a miraculous escape, had been brought here. He lay there looking, to my inexperienced eyes, intensely interesting – his face a mask of gentian violet. I tried a few words of French. No answer but, as I struggled with his lighter (I hadn't learned to smoke) a voice beside me said quite firmly: "Today..." Delighted at this effort to communicate in English, I nodded keenly and, with a bright smile, articulated clearly and fatuously: "Yesterday. " Long pause…then, from the gentian violet depths, the voice repeated: "Yesterday , to-morrow…ke-es me, darling! "

Well, there it was. And how not respond? Needless to say, my slap-dash nursing suddenly took a turn for the better and no man could have had a more responsible, more devoted "special" nurse than this Polish squadron leader. It was positive pleasure to arrive on the ward each day – and in no time I was keenly learning everything I could about Poland and the courageous Poles. "Poly" (as he was known to the whole ward, with some affection) was not as badly burned as was at first feared. He made steady progress and, although periodically a victim of fits of Slavonic gloom, (for which, Heaven knows, there was every reason) he gradually became more sociable generally. The high spots of his life were when members of his Squadron came down to visit him. None of these appeared to have advanced beyond his own initial knowledge of English (though they were all good at that). But their charm and vitality had no difficulty in finding expression and we soon developed an unusual but effective sign-language. I was presented with a history of Poland, which I naturally read avidly and this was followed, I seem to remember, by a recording of Polish folk music. As for the dagger…well the dagger was of course a present from Poly to me. And can you imagine the effect it had on a romantic little V.A.D.?

The day came when I found Poly's bed empty and was told he was up – at the far end of the ward. I looked for him in vain, until the truth began to dawn. Walking slowly towards me was a little dark man. Horrors! It couldn't be true. Romantic Poly, when he joined me, reached barely to my shoulders! The shock was appalling and affects me even now when I think of it.

After that, it was inevitable that, in the convalescent period, he should accompany me each evening to the 'bus. What a pair we must have made – he walking carefully on the (rather high) pavement and I on the road. We used to take a short-cut to the 'bus stop through the town cemetery. I seem to remember the convenience of having a tombstone to sit on while being, very charmingly, embraced…Did I say "tout passe"?

CHAPTER TWO – *Victorian and Edwardian Forebears*

Looking back, my childhood seems dotted here and there with mysterious relations – aunts great and small and ageless cousins, woven into a family fabric quite unintelligible to us – though had I paid attention to the fund of stories my mother let loose on me at times, which utterly bored me, I should have been better equipped to understand them. And yet how many of us ever listen to our mothers' stories, essential as they are to a proper understanding of a family community? To take as an example, the Hambrough family, who, together with other properties, lived partly on the Isle of Wight. I did retain some of their stories as, to people of all ages, they had a dramatic appeal.

In 1828, my mother's great grandfather, John Hambrough, built himself a copy of a medieval castle – crenellated battlements and all – at Ventnor, in the south of the Isle of Wight. The family lived there, on and off, for three generations until a major family tragedy brought an end to a popular small dynasty, interrupted from time to time by visiting friends. (These included Lord Dysart, from whom the Hambroughs originally acquired the land, his guest, Queen Elizabeth of Austria, Queen Victoria from nearby – a friendly neighbour and various other well-known personalities.)

As frequently happened, at a time when infant death in childbirth, or subsequent disease, was all too frequent, many children were born to the Hambroughs, as seen on the Family Tree (see front pages.) William was first married to Charlotte May, with whom, I remember, my mother always felt a mysterious affinity. Indeed, she cherished Charlotte May's inlaid work box, which I inherited. It came with me when I last moved house but I have yet to find it. I seem to remember my mother telling me that Charlotte May had fourteen children, but I have no record of this.

What we do know is that there were five daughters (presumably Charlotte May's) resident at Steephill – where life was joyful in every sense. There seem to have been frequent balls, weddings and so on, and where the opposite sex was concerned, the heir to the Hambrough estate was a seventeen-year-old boy who had just enlisted with the army. There were also, I think, three very small boys (presumably the sons of William's second wife).

Cedric, the heir, was the apple of his father's eye and after he finished school and joined the army, a tutor was engaged for him to take him shooting in Scotland. What happened then became a cause célèbre, a tale of drama, intrigue and, horrifyingly, murder. As far as is known, Cedric was murdered – shot by his tutor, Monson. (See Appendix One.) The crime took place in Scotland where it was recorded as "Case Unproven", so Monson escaped a sentence…

All this was too much for Cedric's father. He had some kind of stroke, lost all his money and became bankrupt. Steephill came on the market and the daughters were suddenly forced out into the real world. None of them had ever worked – indeed, they had had their own lady's maids, and so on. (See Appendix One for an account of this branch of the family.)

It must be said that the Victorians and their successors the Edwardians appear to have had a strong sense of family – to the extent that when disaster struck some members of the family, other members of that family would come forward and, when possible, adopt any child made fatherless.

My maternal grandfather was a high court judge in Rawalpindi (then part of India). My father's family in Liverpool ran many of the clippers trading between the UK and the Far East and his father spent twenty years as a tea merchant in Hangkow. There his four children were born. The children of both families, 'Indian' and 'Chinese', were sent home to England at the age of five, to be looked after by relatives (these tended to be elderly and retired – a world away, literally, for children reared in the Far East.) My mother was devoted to two old aunts, living in Bournemouth.

Although my two sets of grandparents were very different, they both independently made similar decisions to retire very prematurely, to be near their children, whose absence was becoming intolerable for them. Both found homes in what was then apparently an unspoilt village not far from Croydon. I never knew Cumberlands, my mother's much loved home, but it must have been the Victorian sister of Hollybank which we visited as children several times a year. It was thus that my parents met – playing mixed hockey! When I asked my mother one day (as is the wont of children), 'how she fell in love with daddy', she said vaguely, "Oh well, darling, there was this mixed hockey and one day after a storm there was so much mud that it all stuck to the hem of my long black skirt and it began to slip down and your daddy helped me wonderfully. Yes, I think we fell in love with each other then though we didn't marry until a very long time afterwards."

As I said, my paternal grandfather was a merchant in tea in Hangkow. Aunt Ella, my father and their other brother, Arthur and sister, Blanche, spent their early life there. The old man had long since departed this life by the time I was born, but I well remember my grandmother, who died at the ripe old age of 96 when I was 11. Two unmarried daughters and delicate younger son lived at Hollybank, a huge and hideous Victorian house on the edge of London which we visited several times a year – the house, of course, to which my paternal grandfather had retired on leaving China. I can still remember the smell of that house which, when I was a child, used to half fascinate, half repel me. It

Steephill Castle, Isle of Wight

My great grandmother,
Charlotte May, aged about eight

John Hanborough,
one of my Steephill ancestors

was crammed with Chinese bric-a-brac – most of it tasteless and Victorian. The yellow satinwood furniture in the diningroom struck me, even at the age of five, as ugly. In this room the only redeeming feature for us children was the large bowl of canned peaches which invariably stood waiting for us on the sideboard. (Even today the taste of a Californian peach makes me think of Hollybank.)

The younger unmarried sister, Blanche, was, as I remember her, both handsome and capable. We were not allowed to see much of her. She was the Martha of the family -indeed almost a Cinderella figure – who seemed to us children to spend most of her time cake making in the large basement kitchen and rarely joined in any conversation. In contrast, I am told that, from the time she was a young woman, Aunt Ella ruled the family with complete single-mindedness. She was, we were convinced, Chinese. Diminutive and slit-eyed, she possessed skin like yellow parchment and little feet which, I remember hearing, were bound from birth by her ayah.

Luckily for him, my father escaped early from the net. After much travel, he realised that for some time he had been gently falling in love with Amy, shy daughter of the Verners – his parents' neighbours in Kenley. In the approved manner, he presented himself at Cumberlands and asked for her hand in marriage. My maternal grandparents were outraged. What? Allow our daughter to marry someone whose father was in trade? And they a 'County' family? It was inconceivable (the 'County' label may have been justified but only just). My father was sent packing – and in fact joined the Hong Kong and Shanghai Bank, returning unhappily to the land of his birth. He was a keen cricketer and leaving the pitch one day after a successful match was suddenly taken ill. Disseminated sclerosis was diagnosed (now regarded as a form of M.S.) and the doctors gave him five years to live. Poor Edwin was hurriedly sent back to England – a sea voyage which involved three months of stifling discomfort.

I'm thankful to say that my mother's parents then relented. ("Well, poor things," they were heard to say, "Amy will only have five years with him so we had better let them marry").

And marry they did – in Chelsea Old Church. It was 1914 and they honeymooned in the Isle of Wight – returning to their flat in London on the corner of Beaufort Street and the Embankment to find an enormous Zeppelin hanging over the Chelsea Power station across the river. Edwin now walked with one stick and slowly; no question of hurrying down two flights of stairs when the alarm went as it surely would? They camped on the stairs emerging at dawn to find that nothing had changed.

Events conspired to make things far better than expected for the young couple. My mother's family produced a mysterious "Uncle Fred" about whom I know little. My brother and I have searched through the family files (so far in vain) and this is frustrating as we feel we owe our existence to him. Suffice it to say that he appears to have been a wealthy philanthropic bachelor with clusters of Far Eastern tea gardens and rubber plantations 'under his belt'. All we have so far to go on is a large photograph of a youngish man with the family's dark good looks. (His nephew, my Uncle Oliver, was convinced that he himself had Basque blood in his veins.) Uncle Fred took pity on this young couple marrying with at best the prospect of five years ahead of them and virtually no money. As a wedding present he handed over two gifts…a job for my father as General Manager of Tea Gardens and Rubber Estates in South East Asia and an introduction to a

My mother, Amy Verner

My father, Edwin Beazley

Cumberlands in Surrey,
my maternal grandparents' home

My maternal grandmother,
Catherine Verner

remarkable Bacteriologist (one of the first in this country) who in fact gave him twenty years of life, as opposed to five! It was due to Uncle Fred, I'm sure, that our father was able to settle with our mother in East Sussex and drive himself to London in a specially ordered hand-controlled car. It seems appropriate at this stage to say more about my grandmother's family.

Poor Uncle Arthur, our father Edwin's younger brother, led a miserable life. Pronounced too delicate to go to prep or public school, he was kept in cotton wool at home by my grandmother and sent to school locally instead of following Edwin to Repton. Later on, he joined a well-known insurance firm, but appeared permanently disenchanted with his work and, I suspect, made little mark there. Even then, he failed to escape the clutches of my grandmother and aunt – and on family occasions used to hover in the background, ready to execute any dreary chores. We were all fond of Uncle Arthur and my parents suspected him of concealing deep – or perhaps relatively deep – passions beneath a dehydrated exterior. He was a sad man – we felt it even as children.

Lunches at Hollybank always seemed interminable and my grandmother – a little old lady in black, with fine, snow-white hair and (shades of irreverent childhood), a constant drip on the end of her nose – was religiously waited on by Aunt Ella. The meal over, we would repair to the high-ceilinged drawing-room (that indefinable smell everywhere) and Aunt Ella would go to the cupboard below the bookcase. The cupboard was for us a sort of Aladdin's cave, out of which came an astonishing collection of Chinese puzzles – executed in ivory with an almost unbelievable intricacy of carving.

That my aunt was a changeling there could, as I implied earlier, be little doubt, seen through childish eyes. By all accounts my little grandmother was a lady of unimpeachable virtue, and this, therefore, is the only explanation. And yet, and yet. .. I've always been puzzled that such a morally-uplifted lady could have been the recipient of a roll of blue Chinese silk – stolen, according to Aunt Ella (who later presented me with it) from the Peacock Palace during the Boxer Riots. How complicated they were, the Victorians!

My grandmother with
Uncle Arthur and Aunt Ella

Chapter Three – *Growing Up in the 20s and 30s*

On my mother's side, her brother, my Uncle Oliver, was an intriguing mountebank if ever there were one. Before the First World War I remember my mother telling me, he brought a lady friend to spend the weekend with his very Victorian parents. This lady was something of a shock as she sported flaming red hair. After a somewhat difficult weekend my mother travelled back to London with Uncle Oliver and his girlfriend. At a certain moment, it appeared, the girlfriend sprang to her feet, ripped off the red wig and threw it in the rack above their heads. Unfortunately my mother never clarified what lay beneath the wig.

Thereafter Oliver, a High Court judge like his father before him, spent several years in pre-war Cairo where, in what must have been a dizzy round of entertainments, he met and married a beautiful Belgian who, I remember hearing, was the Toast of every Casino within reach. He must have had high linguistic abilities as, in his capacity as High Court Judge, he was frequently taken for an Egyptian. Sadly, though, he and Ninette were – even in the eyes of a small niece – quite incompatible; and when Oliver gave up his job, the two had conflicting ideas as to the future. Instead of moving with a battery of fishing rods to County Cork in Ireland, Ninette insisted they settle close to Cannes, where Casinos were at a premium.

"Matacelle", now part of a well known golf course at Mougins, was a charming verandahed French bungalow; and here, thanks to the generosity of our unpredictable uncle,

Viola Marsden

Matacelle. Ninette and (little Freddy)

13

who hated to see the limitations his brother-in-law's paralysis inflicted on his sister, our family settled for the winter and spring of 1926 and 1927.

Oliver and Ninette had two small children – Freddy and Lorna. They were cared for by Lou-lou, a dashing nineteen-year-old Belgian cousin and I have a vivid memory of her teaching a chuckling two-year-old Freddy the Charleston! (Indeed, I received my second name after her – Ninette). Inevitably the whole first Mediterranean experience has always remained with me: snow on the Alpes Maritime, and mimosa dancing in the wind as Freddy danced with Lou-lou.

My parents settled in the White House, East Sussex, however, and here miraculously, after a long wait, two children had been born to a paraplegic who, some thought, would be incapable of fathering children.

As I describe this near-idyllic scene of our childhood, however, I see I have ignored in an almost Freudian way, an element which was far from being the case. Early on, our parents had become resigned to their inability to conceive, on account of our father's paralysis; and when two small girls were doubly orphaned in our maternal grandmother's family, they agreed to adopt eight-year-old Viola. Her sister, May, two years the elder, had been taken in by our grandmother. These children had had a difficult life, and craved family affection. Freddy and I, of course, had not yet appeared on the scene- but from what I have gathered, there was no problem as far as May was concerned, and she settled easily and happily.

Viola was a different and much more sensitive character. As we see from the photo, she was a worryingly beautiful nine-year-old who longed to be loved, and our handicapped father responded, while our mother, who loved children but who up to then had had little to do with them, was to begin to be inhibited by her usual shyness. This gradually vanished until events took an unexpected turn, with my mother producing two babies in quick succession at the beginning of her forties – a rare achievement in the 1920s. After that Amy's life became focused on myself and Freddy – with Edwin as a benevolent and much-loved husband in the background.

For Viola, who was slowly beginning to settle, it must have been disastrous, and of this period – when Freddy and I were still in the infant and post-infant stage- we knew nothing. Vaguely, so vaguely, we knew that Viola had been sent to a boarding school where she could be in the company of children of her own age. And then suddenly she was back with us again, and it was whispered that she had run away. I knew very little about all this, but was conscious only of a vague feeling of worry about Viola, from which we children were shielded.

Daguerreotype silhouette of my mother

Me aged about five

Portrait of our family in the 1920s

My father with Viola and me (seated below)

For the next few years Viola ran away several times, and it was not until I was, I suppose, about eight years old that I can remember my mother returning from a long search for Viola in London. Remarkably, she had run into her in – was it Tottenham Court Road? Something had given Amy a vague clue which she had followed up; and for a time after that, Viola was with us at Parrock Wood, where we moved after ten years or so. Then she vanished and I remember that my father was distraught. After a time a letter came, enclosing a photo of a now ash-blonde Viola. It appeared that she had joined some drama group at Denham studios, and there was also a photo of an Australian actor who intended taking her back to his homeland. I always remember my father's horror, especially when he remarked that, as far as he could see, the man in question only had one ear.

The blondly beautiful Viola came to say goodbye, which was painful for everyone, especially my father. I think two or three letters were received with her new address, at least one of which was written to May, her sister. The war had broken out, and my father was very nearly at the end of his life. After his death, it was found that he had left Viola a considerable inheritance, and her bank was contacted. The bank finally acknowledged this communication, and eventually confirmed that she had collected her inheritance. But the expected letter to my mother never appeared. Her sister May contacted me when I was next in England with news of Viola's death.

As far as Oliver and Ninette were concerned, life in Cannes proceeded with little hint of an approaching family tragedy which was to have a similar impact on our family life. One thing was already painfully obvious, however. His parents adored Freddy, a little charmer who unquestionably bound them together. For Lorna they had no use- and worse, went out of their way to favour me rather than her – a painful situation.

Thereafter, news of that family became scarce and for some time our Sussex life moved on in other directions. We did learn though that, four years later, the family fell apart after Little Freddy's early death from leukaemia, aged six. (He was called Little Freddy because he shared my brother's name, both boys having been given the name of a much loved young uncle who was killed in the Great War.) Ninette absconded with her boyfriend-of-the-time who very quickly deserted her, and Uncle Oliver landed on my ever welcoming mother in a state of complete collapse.

Amy, our mother, agonised to see Oliver's total grief at Little Freddy's death, and hoped to rehabilitate him, at any rate partially, in the bosom of her comfortable, loving family. Meanwhile, Oliver's only desire was to make contact with his son through spiritualism – i.e. beyond the grave. From then on his life was dominated by this goal – though not long afterwards he married again. Mary was very Irish. Half Oliver's age and

Mavis Freddy & Edwin picnic c 1927

Freddy and me around 1930

the antithesis of Ninette! Her pregnancy produced another daughter, and ultimately they moved to the Channel Isles where, we understood, Uncle Oliver conducted a clandestine – but to him highly satisfactory – trade in crabs! Meanwhile Lorna had settled permanently with us – first at the White House and later at Parrock Wood, since she was totally neglected by her parents. Early on in his second marriage, Oliver and Mary moved to a Devonshire village near Exeter. He settled into a routine whereby a medium known to him came once a week and conducted a séance with Freddy and other people in the family who had "passed on".

Once a year, our parents took us children on holiday to a farmhouse in Dartmoor – and this meant that once a year we paid a visit to Uncle Oliver and Mary. This visit was dreaded by us all for it appeared that the house was heavily haunted – and indeed, as Mary confided to our mother, an attempt to repair the faulty lighting system drove the local electrician from the house. Later, just at the sensitive time of puberty, Lorna was forced to attend séances – and as a result had a major breakdown.

Before leaving my uncle, it seems appropriate to mention his genuine desire to help when I first went to my boarding school. Lorna had already been there a term and though I was anxious in one way to join her there, I was partly terrified of being unpopular with the other girls. Uncle Oliver read me a lecture, saying he had managed to buy in Ireland a remarkable mixture which, when spread on a chair, proceeded to turn the next occupier red hot and then icy cold in a very sensitive place. It had a particularly evil smell. "That", he announced with conviction, "will unquestionably make you the most popular girl in your House." I duly packed the small phial he gave me in my old-fashioned trunk, and off we went to the Beehive. I will not dwell on what followed. Suffice it to say that the precious elixir broke in my trunk -and the ensuing smell permeated my clothes, my room which I shared with an unlucky girl of the name of Monica, and ultimately the whole House.

It is worth recording that Lorna (who was in another House) suffered no such problems. Her father, being totally uninterested in her, had not thought of trying to alleviate any problems she might have. I have luke-warm memories of the Beehive school, academically. It did have, however, a remarkable French Mademoiselle, who saw to it that Beehive girls had outstanding successes in French. (Not much else though.)

My brother Freddy left home (aged eight) to join his prep school at Rottingdean. St Aubyns was run by Mr Layng, a wise and charming man who sized up his pupils with his own form of psychotherapy and was loved by them. They were boys from mixed families and many went on to Eton. "Mr" Layng had a particular interest in Stowe, the new public

Left to right: Lorna, Anne Bowden-Smith, 'D' Bowden-Smith, my mother, me and Geoffrey at Parrock Wood

Family picnic in the 1930s

'Puck' and me at Parrock Wood

Lorna, Freddy and me at a family wedding

school under the leadership of J.F. Roxburgh (known affectionately to all as J.F.). Mr Layng was keen that Freddy, who already showed promise of becoming an outstanding young athlete, should become one of his pupils, and so it was. I missed Freddy of course but the arrival of Lorna put another aspect on things.

Looking back over all these years my brother Freddy and I find we share the same sun-filled memories of our own early childhood home – the little pink-and-white Sussex house, its garden carefully sheltered by box hedges, the solid cart-horse, Dobbin, who took us for rides in the pony-trap; tea time under the huge oak tree which served as a kind of garden umbrella, the smell of newly-mown grass, which was wonderful for making elves' houses when the gardener wasn't looking; and in summer (but surely it was always summer in those days?) the beguiling scents of honeysuckle and summer flowering jasmine creeping through our bedroom window. Tea was always brought by our adored Nannie, Margaret, and we picnicked with toys and sandwiches beneath the huge oak tree and savoured strawberries and cream eaten in hay nests. How spoiled, how wonderfully shielded, we two were!

The White House…the very name brings with it a kaleidoscope of memories. I remember the day they replaced our brown hip bath with a modern white enamel one. Another image is of my brother Freddy, aged four-ish, conducting our ancient Aunt Ella round the garden and showing off. ("I can remember going down to be born in the pony-trap.") Another unforgettable memory was when we found an Elephant Hawk Moth in the fuschia bed.

My father played our upright piano entirely by ear. His selection of compositions was made chiefly for Freddy and myself. The fact that they were inevitably of a low-brow choice delighted us – and as I write I see and hear quite clearly something I haven't thought of in at least seventy years. Daddy is seated at the piano and "vamping" one of our favourites –

"A long time ago, I remember it well,
A beautiful maid in the village did dwell.
She dwelt all alone with her father, serene;
Her age it was red and her hair was nineteen."

(The last line, of course, always convulsed us.) Above the piano hung a copy of a picture of 'Cherry Ripe' by a painter unknown. Our mother doted on it and seemed positively to draw inspiration from the demure little figure. Imagine therefore the shock to her when one morning she glanced as usual at the source of her inspiration and found

Our childhood home – The White House

her darling heavily adorned with black moustache and eyebrows with a roguish look in what had once been an innocent eye. Our mother exploded, we children rocked about in near hysteria and Daddy smiled faintly but (we were sure) approvingly. I need hardly say that this was during one of Uncle Oliver's visits.

We were conscious of our beloved father's increasing disability and my earliest mental picture of him walking with one stick was gradually replaced by one of him with two. Occasionally we were taken on trips with him to his office in Great William Street, in the City. Once Edwin could no longer manage his hand-controlled car, however, there followed a succession of chauffeurs, mostly very helpful. I hated these trips because in those days Great William Street was close to some breweries – and dray-horses would laboriously drag the beer barrels up the steep road, bringing with them the (to me) revolting smell of beer. It made me car-sick.

The White House was a comfortable household – run by a cook, parlourmaid and housemaid. There was also Nannie Margaret in the early years. Margaret was destined to become a nurse at St. Thomas's Hospital. She had lost her guardian (the Mother Superior at East Grinstead convent) after she had been with us for five years. Before dying,

Sister Frances had begged our mother to take her place as guardian and this happened quite naturally as she and our mother were devoted to each other and Margaret was loved by us all. The time of her leaving us was deferred for two or three years and when it took place our mother acted in loco parentis. An account of her remarkable life is separately described in this volume. (Page 112, 'Margaret's Story').

My brother and I went to little Dane school in Forest Row, not far from the weekend cottage where A.A. Milne and his family spent their weekends. One day A.A. Milne brought his small son there – Christopher Robin himself – saying there was to be a big pageant of Ashdown Forest which would include a "Christopher Robin" episode. His son was to meet our little group and decide which of us would best play the part of Christopher Robin's animals. My brother and I were given the shared part of Kanga, alternating in a hot smelly skin during the week of the pageant. Subsequently, it was announced that the Duchess of York, later Queen Elizabeth, the Queen Mother, was to visit our pageant. I remember that my brother and I fought as to who should have the honour to act in front of her. I tossed a coin and won, which my brother Freddy thought grossly unfair and I presented the Duchess with a bouquet of flowers.

(Seventy years went by. John and I had retired in Hampshire and by chance I discovered, amazingly, that a new musical friend of ours had been at our Dane School with us. She assured me that from the age of six she had been in love with my brother, and hoped he was still alive. I assured her he was and brought them together, without spectacular success.

In December 2001 Daphne, as she was called, rang me one lunchtime in a state of high excitement.

"Mavis! I've just seen both of us."

"Poor thing" I thought to myself "…must have had a 'senior' moment."

However, it turned out she had in fact seen a BBC documentary commemorating Christopher Robin's death and showing what must have been the first video showing what must have been one of the first non-silent movies ever. It showed the AA Milne production at the 1929 Ashdown Forest pageant and there were Freddy and me in a single skin playing Kanga!. "And there we were," said Daphne, "you, Kanga, striding through long grass, and me as Wol, trotting along beside you. I phoned the BBC at once, of course, and told them about us." This was the last thing I would have dreamed of doing, but I listened as she described the BBC's (apparent) delighted reaction, and the fact that three producers would be arriving at my house at three-thirty to register our antediluvian reaction to seeing ourselves all of seventy years ago. I had an appointment with the dentist at three-thirty

Freddy and me with my father and 'Dobbin'

Uncle Oliver, Ninette and Lorna with little Freddy (in pram)

and had the immense satisfaction of saying to them, on arrival at the surgery,

"I can't stay long – the BBC are waiting for me."

The resultant transmission was apparently so successful that the BBC repeated the performance the following May, by which time others had come out of the woodwork: Eyore, predictably, from the New Forest, Piglet from Wiltshire, and Pooh, who oddly enough seemed to have emigrated to Yorkshire. After each transmission the phone rang endlessly and the greeting "Hi, Kanga!" rapidly ceased to be amusing. Throughout the whole period I found myself drawn back into childhood and far further back in terms of roots.

When I was about ten, to our surprise and, indeed, shock, our parents announced their intention to move house. What? Leave our treasured White House? Impossible! And the fact that soon there would scarcely be room for a growing family scarcely seemed relevant to us children. And as for Daddy confessing he had fallen in love with Parrock Wood – a much larger house belonging to one of his friends, with a beautiful terraced garden running down a hill…we didn't want to know.

"There's a wonderful room for you, Babs," (my name in the family), "and we know you are going to love it…" etc, etc. One thing was clear. Our parents had gone mad. This pearl of perfection was on the edge of Ashdown Forest, with a beautiful view.

I cannot remember the transition period, only that Parrock Wood quite rapidly

Me in the late 1930s

inspired another love of a more mature kind. I remember vividly, though, that the spectre of World War Two dominated all adult thought and conversation, while at the Beehive school, the German national anthem was not infrequently played in chapel as a hymn tune. The Nazi-worshipping young German teacher would stand stiffly each time at the Nazi salute, to our complete mystification.

1938 to 1939 was a hard period for my mother. Our father was becoming increasingly frail and it was more and more difficult to find staff to run a medium-sized house. The international news was becoming worryingly tense, especially tense, especially in Austria, where Austrian Jews and their families were being systematically apprehended. I arrived home for the summer holidays, to find that my Mama had made one of her practical decisions, whereby she had offered refugee status to four Austrians in return for their help in running our house – Parrock Wood.

I well remember my first meeting with Else Neschling, in our largish kitchen. My Mama was distinctly nervous as she introduced me to our new cook who was instantly and naturally determined to explain that she was the daughter of a prominent Viennese doctor. It quickly became evident that such German as Mama had long ago acquired in

Dresden as a girl had deserted her. Politely but feebly, she endeavoured to tell Else that we quite understood, but at the same time were determined to have practical assistance on the culinary side. What would she be dishing up were we to be lunching today in Vienna?

"Naturally everyone loves Viennese food, and we are looking forward to trying out your ideas…" The profound silence which followed was punctuated by an apparently defiant: "In Vienna we eat MICE." (Maize!) As for the other three Austrians, the embittered 'parlourmaid ' and her daughter stayed only a few weeks, as did the housemaid who walked in a dream. This was doubtless because they found the change in their status degrading. Else, however, eventually remained with our mother for twenty years, establishing a love hate relationship which affected us all.

In April 1940 Hitler prepared to invade Britain. At this moment our father died, and Aunt Dorothy, a close sister of my Mama, came up from Devon for the funeral. Aunt Dorothy, who lived with a very elderly husband 'Uncle John' whom she'd recently married in a sprawling Georgian house in Tavistock, was generously loading it with friends and relations expected to be in the path of invasion. It was decided that the three of us (my brother Freddy (now eighteen), my mother and myself) should join her as soon as possible and we began packing up the house, warning the police that Else would be in charge.

Finding one's way across England at that time was quite a challenge. No signposts

Lorna and me as bridesmaids (right) at Aunt Dorothy and Uncle John's wedding

of any kind, and constant road-blocks to throw you off track. For my brother and me, and even for our entrepreneurial Mama, it provided considerable excitement, and our eventual arrival at Tavistock felt quite like a victory.

It makes me blush to think how thoughtlessly we abandoned Else to the wolves. A few days later she phoned in hysteria to say that the police had accused her of signalling to an enemy plane from her attic bedroom. The stolid Sussex police were themselves deeply suspicious of her, and it was scarcely a wonder. She looked unquestionably and, they felt, disturbingly like a German, and showed distinct signs of being a double agent. She also acted as if she was absurdly stupid and looked the part.

Well, our family stayed down in Tavistock till late summer. History meanwhile evolved around us and we were particularly caught up in it during the Dunkirk retreat when the fate of our aunt's much loved nephew Eardley was unknown. He came through – as did a large part of the Expeditionary Force – thanks to the heroic rescue efforts of ordinary Englishmen with ordinary small boats. This, although principally a national disaster, made us burst with pride.

When our father died, as described earlier, our aunt Dorothy had come up from Tavistock for the funeral. She and Amy, our mother, were very close to each other, and as an invasion by Hitler was at that moment considered a matter of time, it was arranged that Freddy, Amy and I should begin packing up Parrock Wood before joining Dorothy and her husband in Devon. This we did and again, as planned at the beginning of September, 1940. Freddy became eligible for an aeronautical course – leading on to a training as a fighter pilot in the RAF. His training was to take place in Florida, we learnt, rather to our surprise. (America had only recently declared her hand in favour of the Allies.) We were told the date of his departure, and Amy and I booked a double room for the night before in a small hotel in Hindhead. (I have a recollection of a crowded little hotel ; very evidently there was a gathering of families.) I should say that Aunt Dorothy had earlier made plans to move to New Zealand where we had cousins. She and Uncle John, being childless, had adopted a boy, Dick, who had early on shown signs of acute nervousness to the point where a consultant psychiatrist had warned Dorothy that he should at all costs be removed from the United Kingdom, into a quieter environment. (Bombing had started to show signs of acceleration.) Dorothy had gone through the loss of her younger brother in the First World War – another Freddy – to whom she was devoted. They were very close in age, and this Freddy from all accounts was a remarkable, rather latter-day version of Rupert Brooke, adored by his family, and an outstanding all-rounder at Oxford, though no poet.

Anne Bowden-Smith with me in 1941

Mt. Tavey House near Tavistock - Aunt Dorothy's home
– where Freddy and I went with my mother in 1940

Sybil Verner (see Appendix 1) came into my mother's family when Steephill collapsed. She was much loved and, as can be seen, inseparable from my mother, who was exactly the same age. After Amy's marriage, Dorothy also grew very close to Sybil – and a thunderbolt fell when Sybil contracted cancer, and died in our home, the White House.

Dorothy's marriage to the much older Uncle John had promised companionship but nothing else. And to remove any sign of romance, she contracted diphtheria during the ceremony. The latter took place at the Queen's Chapel of the Savoy, with a lovely procession of bridesmaids, of which Lorna and I were part.

I well remember how Dorothy hated the whole idea of going to New Zealand (thereby separating herself from the remainder of those she loved) and particularly parting with Amy who she felt badly needed her.

Anyway, at the little hotel I was woken from a deep sleep and there was our mother in shock. She was sitting on the edge of my bed, crying her eyes out. All I could make out was that she had had a dream, a terrible dream. In her dream she had seen an old man standing next to a grave and she knew that Dorothy was dead. When later a note arrived from her brother-in-law, enclosing a photo of the grave, she saw it was exactly the same as what she had seen in the dream.

There had often, oddly, been a sense of the occult in the Hambrough family. I remember my mother telling me that she had a dream at Cumberlands, where she and Edwin (recently married) had been staying the weekend. In her dream she was going down to breakfast, passing a chest of drawers on a landing. There was a silver salver there where waiting letters were placed. To her horror she had seen a sealed blue envelope there. "And I knew Freddy (Oliver's brother) was dead." They had sent the usual blue telegram which we all dreaded. Sure enough, it arrived – and the family never recovered from its news.

Meanwhile, my brother Freddy left us to join the Aeronautical College in London, before being eligible for the RAF. I signed up for Red Cross training at the Tavistock hospital, and Mount Tavy, our aunt's house, filled with English engineers who had somehow become stranded in Brittany.

In early September I had finished my short training, and Mama and I returned to East Sussex, to Else's immense relief. I was reunited at this point with Anne Bowden-Smith. I had earlier completed an inadequate Red Cross Training with her, and we were now given the necessary but uninspiring task of helping to "settle" some completely miserable East-London evacuees.

One afternoon, in the middle of the Blitz – by this time we were working at East Grinstead Hospital, I came off duty and met my mother in town. We then called in to see Aunt Ella who, with her bachelor younger brother Uncle Arthur, now occupied a small house in a neighbouring village. By 1941, when my mother and I went to have tea that afternoon, my grandmother had of course long since been dead. Hollybank had been sold, and the aunts had moved to this small house near East Grinstead, with the inspiring name of Lavengro. (Nobody could have been less gypsy-Iike than its new inmates). Uncle Arthur now lived in London during the week, but used to join them lugubriously at weekends. Aunt Blanche had alas developed pneumonia too soon to be able to benefit from the discovery of penicillin, and had died – unnecessarily, it seemed – in the late '30s. At this moment Uncle Arthur was on the point of retirement and, according to my parents, was cherishing a secret plan to live most of the year at Menton, in the south of France, where he had occasionally visited cousins. Aunt Ella's strength of personality immediately came into play, however, and (with unrefined autocracy) she issued a royal command, to the effect that his duty lay in moving in to look after her. I remember Uncle Arthur at this stage. He was like a worm, wriggling desperately to escape Aunt Ella's predatory beak. Needless to say, he was unsuccessful – and settled down at Lavengro as her stooge.

Well, on this particular afternoon, we had hardly bent over our teacups (full of their special blend of Dooars China tea presumably marketed by my grandfather) when the air-raid warning sounded. This was so much part of life at that time that my mother and I took no notice and, both being attached to our food, began attacking the cake. Uncle Arthur, however, was on his feet in a trice. From some mysterious recess he produced a series of hardboard shutters, and began hurriedly fitting them into prepared slots in front of the windows. The place was plunged into darkness, I remember, but we were forbidden

Freddy in his RAF uniform

My brother Freddy with Lancaster bomber and crew in the war

to put on the light. Panting slightly, he then ushered us into the tiny hall where, under the staircase, he had placed three deck chairs. (No, two. One was permanently there, as apparently Aunt Ella slept in it every night.) We were motioned to these seats, whereupon Uncle Arthur shot into the kitchen, returning in a moment with three enamel washing-up bowls, which he instructed us to invert on our heads. Not daring to look at each other, we obeyed him -only to discover that they still contained water. This was too much, and we both collapsed into giggles, to the keen disapproval of Aunt Ella. Meanwhile, Uncle Arthur was urgently searching for something upstairs. Like a squirrel who has alighted on hidden nuts, he descended triumphantly, with earplugs for all of us.

Laughter was not untinged with compassion, (and some shame) as later on we made our way home in the 'bus. The last straw, I'm afraid, had been the discovery that Uncle Arthur kept a German dictionary at the ready…under the stairs.

My Aunt Ella in the 1940s

(Footnote: obstinate though she was to the rest of her family, Aunt Ella was affection itself to her only nephew and niece. Surprisingly, there was an element of the maternal in her, which helped perhaps to explain why (to the irritation of my mother) she was for years a member of the village Mothers Union. As for Uncle Arthur, the poor timid little chap was the soul of desiccated kindness. Freud would probably have been fascinated by him).

CHAPTER FOUR – *Second World War*

During the last years of the 1930s, my parents and I seemed to spend strained times in their bedroom, listening to the Prime Ministers' voices, and attempting to stimulate our 'Faith Buds'. I can see us now, gathered round Edwin's bed and our rather shabby wireless, listening intently to Chamberlain's explanation on his return from his visit to Hitler in Berchesgarten.

"I bring you Peace in our Time"…It sounded comforting and, God knows, we all needed comfort in the face of an inherent cynicism where the older generation was concerned.

And then, unforgettably, Baldwin – by this time, Prime Minister –stunned us all in a voice which he had difficulty in controlling, with the news that the King, Edward VIII, was about to abdicate, in order that he could then marry the American, Mrs Simpson. Oh, those were hard, unthinkable days.

The spectre of the Second World War continued to haunt us and, while Freddy and I found the endless conversation on the issue intensely boring, we also felt faintly scared.

The East London evacuees, whom Anne and I were to help re-settle, consisted of several hundred unfortunate children who had been separated from their parents at London railway stations and conveyed to places considered to be safer than their homes. Our group had been sent to Forest Row village hall. Many of them were hysterical. The Red Cross's job and therefore ours was to find them temporary homes. Tension everywhere was unbearable and I well remember, as one of many teenage recruits, feeling hopelessly ill-equipped to handle the effects of the trauma experienced by these children. We moved with them to a large impersonal house in the village where they were to be cared for.

I was in the village hall at Forest Row when I heard the announcement that we had declared war against Germany. At the time I was with a Swiss girl whose mother ran a finishing school. We were both horribly aware of the meaning of war and broke down in floods of tears. At this stage I had, of course, never met my future husband. He was then 'Resident Clerk' at the Foreign Office and it was in that capacity, I was later to learn that, amazingly, he had the task of despatching the telegram containing the declaration of war, to Berlin.

It was the following year that we were transferred to East Grinstead Hospital and the Battle of Britain exploded around us. I was assigned to the ward dealing with severe burns and, as I have already said, it was here that I met Sq. Leader Krasnodemski. The work was as fascinating as it was character-forming, but not unnaturally often it was gruesome. We were visited by the Red Cross to ensure that the demands placed on voluntary teenagers were not excessive.

I suppose I started work at the Foreign Office about the time the fire-bomb blitz occurred. Slightly, but only slightly, less ingenue by this time, I entered as practically the lowest form of life, and after three months was promoted to be assistant to Gladwyn Jebb's PA. Gladwyn was at this time head of the Post-War Reconstruction department which, together with the Archives and the Resident Clerks' flat, occupied the top floor of the Foreign Office. Being Gladwyn, he managed to create within his (and everyone else's) as yet theoretical terms of reference, a hive of turmoil and activity, and it is a tribute to the man that he was in close touch with all Cabinet decisions of the moment, let alone policy planning.

Miss Ayres, his PA, was a distinguished lady in the Foreign Office hierarchy – second only, I seem to remember, to the PA to the Permanent Under- Secretary, Sir Orme Sargent (alias Moley). On the day I made my debut in that office she seemed to me Methuselah himself – and indeed she was all of 36, which speaks for itself. Aphrodite had clearly passed her by. However, she had an excellent brain – acknowledged by high office standing – and must have been a first-class PA. How baffled the poor woman must have felt by the immaturity of her new assistant. The situation was quickly aggravated by the fact that, in those giddy, mid-war days, I was out every night – while her own life was clearly pedestrian in the extreme. Gladwyn normally worked long hours, and we took it in turns to stay late. I must have infuriated her by my frequent demands to change late duty with her; for it was only too clear that I did not thus upset her own 'dates'.

One day, however, I arrived late as usual, and found her transformed – glowing, one would almost say. On the desk in front of her was a jewel case. She opened it, asking me to admire what she had just received from ' a friend'. Inside was a string of, I suppose, rather beautiful amber beads. I have never liked them, so am no judge. With half a sigh she murmured: "Of course I'd rather they had been pearls, but all the same… " After that, she would from time to time introduce her 'friend's' name into conversation. I understood he was a journalist – Eurasian – and that they met fairly often.

One Monday morning, I arrived at the office to find it empty. This was surprising, as Gwen was always installed at her desk by the time I arrived. I waited, but there was no sign of her or anyone else. Gladwyn Jebb., I knew, should be arriving at any moment, and suddenly I wondered if she could be ill. There was a disturbing silence everywhere… After nearly an hour, Gladwyn's political 'No. 2' arrived, looking rather like a ghost. "Miss Beazley," he said agitatedly, "leave everything, will you, and come and help me with an urgent task?" He opened the door of the cupboard where we kept our files of Top Secret

Cabinet Papers. These contained every current Cabinet Paper of importance – for Gladwyn had earlier managed to convince those concerned that, in his capacity as Head of the Post-War Reconstruction Department, he must have access to the most Top Secret documents. "We must go through each file meticulously, Miss Beazley, and remove any paper which we see has been folded in four." Jim Lambert mopped his brow, which was covered in beads of sweat. "Come! There's no time to lose…" At the end of an hour, we had still not quite finished; and on the floor besides us was a pile of Cabinet Papers, all marked "Top Secret" – all with marks of having been folded in four.

Gladwyn appeared half way through the morning. He looked somehow different, his usually completely confident figure seeming to walk on cotton wool legs. Eventually, he summoned me next door, and told me what had happened. Apparently MI5 had been becoming increasingly worried by the content of certain articles appearing each Sunday in "The People". These sometimes contained Top Secret information known only to members of the Cabinet and recipients of Cabinet Papers, and it was realised there must be a leak somewhere. Eventually, they succeeded in narrowing the field dramatically, and, the day before the one I am describing, MI5 closed in on Gwen in the lunch-hour, as she was walking through the park on her way back from her 'friends' flat. They caught her red-handed – with two Cabinet Papers, folded into four, in her briefcase.

This story is painfully tragic. Also, surely, it illustrates the impossibility of guarding against the frailty of human nature. Months after, when the two were brought to trial – she from Holloway, he from Wormwood Scrubs – they faced each other for the first time since the event. MI5 had long since discovered that there was no question of secrets being intentionally passed to the enemy but rather, a case of personal ambition (amounting to megalomania) on the part of the journalist. Indeed, in his defence he declared that he had conceived it his duty to enlighten the public on matters about which they were being kept in the dark. When questioned about his feelings concerning Gwen, he looked across at her homely and (by now) ravaged face, and burst into derisive laughter.

I seem to remember that she received three years hard labour – mitigated to 18 months for good conduct. Some years later, I received a short note from her. By this time I was married, and we were in Paris. She wrote to say that she had heard this through a close friend of hers on the Embassy staff. It was good to know, she went on, that some people were lucky in life. For herself, she had been out of prison for a couple of years, and was living with her old father in Sussex. The days went by very quietly… there wasn't much to live for.

The pay, I remember, was appallingly bad at the Foreign Office, and this applied to all ranks. We were told, when we went for our interviews, that 'the interest of the work more than compensated for low salaries'. To a certain extent this was true, but you had to live, and there were also those who – less lucky than myself and my cousin Lorna, who shared 'digs' with me – had no allowance of their own to supplement their pay-packet. Lorna and I lived first in two bed-sitters at the top of an Oakley Street boarding house, and later – more respectably – at a hostel called

St Paul's Cathedral in flames during the Blitz of World War Two

The Grubbery. This was ideally situated, as we were only 20 yards from the Underground at South Kensington. (I also knew one of the resident clerks at the Foreign Office whom indeed I ended up marrying. Their flat turned out to be very conveniently placed for a nightcap on our way home, so to speak).

Our social life was pretty full – particularly every weekend, when we went home to Sussex. (My mother kept 'Open House' for members of a Canadian regiment stationed nearby). On free nights we washed our hair, played the gramophone and read aloud from Donne, our great passion. Yet the war was never far from our minds, and each night my mother quietly watched the great red glow in the sky to the north from her top floor window, knowing that London was burning and wondering how close to Freddy and me the flames were licking.

Every eleventh night we were on Fire Duty at the Foreign Office – a chore which we detested on account of its discomforts, but which also had its compensations. We were all 'bedded down' in the bowels of the building, in narrow, acutely uncomfortable bunks. There was no air, and I for one could never sleep. However, we weren't there much of the time, as the moment the air-raid warning sounded, we donned our fire helmets and swarmed upstairs to the roof. The raid would have just started, and high above us a raider was caught in the searchlight beams. All round us the 'ack-ack' guns opened up. The German plane managed to elude the beams… was picked out again by them… 'Ack-ack' flack began spattering the part of the roof where we stood. "Keep down, you fools," a voice shouted. "you'll only get hit." But something kept us standing there. It was movingly beautiful…and we – we, after all, belonged to the people who never got hit. Below us, the lake in the park gleamed dimly. The pelicans and other water birds which roosted on the island hated the noise and never got used to it. They stirred, uttered the sounds of other, far-distant climes, flapped their wings. On the way in from the country, after a particularly hard night, we passed some badly hit shops with "Open as usual" scrawled over one of them, while next door a worse damaged greengrocers carried the message "More open than usual!" Cockney humour flourished, even in the Blitz.

"…You'll be flying unusually high, as German planes are out over the Bay of Biscay. The MO will give you a briefing…" The Station Commander saluted, and left us to Fl. Lt. Peters. The Germans, we were told, knew about our movements and were combing the Bay of Biscay. As a result, our unpressurised Liberator would be obliged to fly higher than it was equipped to do. We were warned about earache and told us how to cope with it. Then we filed out of the RAF hut. It was just possible to make out the Liberator plane – crouching like a shadowy monster in the black-out and pre-dawn gloom.

It was the winter of 1943 and the Moscow Conference had taken place in October. John, Resident Clerk and Head of Economics in Gladwyn's department, was on this conference, and just before the party left, we became engaged. We decided to make it public as soon as he returned from Moscow, and this we did. Oliver Harvey, PPS to Anthony Eden, and Maudie his wife gave an impromptu small party for us, and it was next morning when Gladwyn threw his bombshell. He approached John and told him he himself was about to go on a further high-level Four Power meeting, and said he wished to take me too. I was given a day, and a new book of clothing coupons, to outfit myself. It seemed the destination might be warm, with cold nights.

The following evening the party, consisting of Sir Anthony Eden and his senior Generals, boarded the train at Paddington. Lights were dim inside the carriages, curtains were drawn. John came to see us off – rather unsatisfactorily for him, as I was far too excited to respond to newly-engaged ardour.

And now here we were – boarding the aircraft! Liberators in war-time were hardly beds of roses. On this occasion, however, the 'plane was specially fitted out with one – a curtained bunk for the comfort of the Foreign Secretary. As we began taking our seats he announced categorically that he'd no intention of using it, and ordered his PA, Barbara May, to climb in. Barbara, luckily for her, was able to pass the buck; and it fell to me, Lowest Form of Life on board, to replace the Great Man in that bed… I crouched miserably on top of the blankets, in the shame of knowing myself excluded from the fraternity of bucket-seats, now occupied by Major-Generals. From time to time, as the night wore on, I pushed aside the curtains and gazed out. It was the first time I had ever flown. Where, one wondered with interest, were all those enemy fighters? The neutral lights of Lisbon were, to all those who had led a mole-like existence for four years, both a memory and a promise. It seemed unbelievable that, far below, life was proceeding unfurtively, lit up for all to see. And yet, how many spy-networks were in fact thriving in all that flamboyance?

At 6 a.m. we landed at Gibraltar. Early morning sunshine flooded the Rock. The Mediterranean washed it caressingly. Barbara and I shared a room in a small hotel near Government House. Still we did not know our destination, though Barbara clearly had some inkling. We spent the day shopping for long-forgotten luxuries like bananas, visiting the monkeys on the Rock, having tea (or did we?) at Government House. By 5am next morning we were on our way to the plane again. It was getting light and by the time we had crossed the Mediterranean there was bright sunshine. All that day we flew eastwards, over the North African desert – passing, at one stage, clear evidence in the sand of 8th Army traces. More macabre, we saw also the wreck of a Liberator scattered over the desert. Sunset was dying the distance blue and desert-rose when we flew into Cairo Airport. Jaded and a bit dazed, we were driven to our various lodgings. Our VIPs were spirited away to the Embassy, and Barbara and I despatched to the Junior Officers' Club.

The next few days were spent partly in Cairo and mostly at Mena House, in the desert next to the Pyramids just outside Cairo, where the conference took place. My own memories of them are kaleidoscopic: the sights and smells (above all the smells) of Islam – so alien to an island-bound Anglo-Saxon; the mosques of a beauty and cultural strangeness which at that time was disturbing; the poverty and sickness (old men parading bleeding leg-stumps as they begged in crowded streets); the ancient world outside the windows at Mena House – seeming to contemplate us with a wisdom so infinite that at times one felt like a bee who had somehow strayed into the beard of Allah. Memories of General Smuts on the steps of the Embassy – lean, tanned, with blazing blue eyes, those overwhelming Pyramids, Roosevelt in his wheel-chair, Churchill's frog-like figure. Also, dinner with Charles Johnson, old friend and colleague of John's, and his fascinating Russian wife Natasha – with their amazing and at that time still youthful Egyptian servant Mo, waiting on us. An afternoon at the Gezira Club; drinks at Shepherd's Hotel (already run-down and flea-ridden).

Rumours of another, even more secret, conference. Stalin was expected to join this one. The British delegation on this occasion would be substantially smaller. No chance for the likes of me! And then, Gladwyn proving true to form – his message to me to be ready to leave next morning. This time we travelled in a Dakota 'plane – a long, bumpy flight, which took us over the Holy Land, over the Tigris and Euphrates towards Iran.

We had by now guessed our destination. I found myself next to a small, fair WREN – a detachment of whom were being brought along as de-coders. At one stage, as we flew high above the desert to avoid bumping, she collapsed for lack of oxygen, and had to be revived.

Tehran at the beginning of December, 1943, presented a scene of sharp contrasts – as it surely still does today. Here, western culture slid into the beckoning East. Open drains ran along the streets (you had to jump over them to reach the small 'Aladdin' shops), sophisticated villas with walled gardens filled with formal flower-beds stood nearby. Warm, sunny temperatures by day were followed by freezing nights. The impressive avenue of poplars leading into the city was flanked by Mount Demavend's snow-topped dome.

Once again, Ministers and senior officials were wafted to our Legation. It soon became clear, though, that the arrival of ten WRENS and two FO secretaries had not been bargained for. Eventually, the YWCA nobly opened its doors to us, and provided a red-blanketed dormitory, with "Valor" oil stoves to contend with bitter nights.

The British Legation (which after the war became of course an Embassy) must be one of the most charming and habitable of ambassadorial buildings we have. As I remember it, a long, creeper-covered veranda ran the whole length of the house, leading into a high-walled garden which seemed a riot of colour. The Buffs, who had been hastily summoned from Basra to guard the building during the conference, were in evidence everywhere. The house had been quickly turned into offices and conference-rooms – as had also, one presumes, the Russian, Chinese and American Legations.

Most of the Legation staff lived in the compound. The bachelor commercial counsellor and his sister were, I remember, wonderfully hospitable with hot baths – a luxury not to be had at the YWCA. Once again, I have a kaleidoscopic memory of those few days: shopping for Persian miniatures; visiting the Gulestan Palace (an over-ornate Palace which screamed bad taste) picnicking at Gulahek, where the Legation always moved for the summer; forgetting for one brief – very brief – moment that I was newly-engaged; watching the guests turn up for Churchill's birthday party. The high spot here was the arrival of Stalin. Like a small boy at a party (he was a surprisingly little man), he stood in the Legation hall surrounded by burly Russian Generals – waiting for someone to relieve him of his coat. The Russian High Command all had their right hands in their pockets. We were sure they were nervously clutching grenades.

And then, we were on our way home – with a 24-hour stop at Cairo to tie up loose ends. We flew this time at night over the North African desert. Towards morning, it became evident that the pilot was having some kind of trouble. Eventually, we were told that two out of three of the plane engines had gone dead. We should have to make an emergency

General Smuts

The Nile near Cairo

landing, at Algiers.

Harold Macmillan, at that time Minister resident in Algiers, can hardly have dreamed, when he got up that morning that his Foreign Secretary would be having breakfast with him. So it was however, and I remember, at about 9am, our whole dishevelled party sitting on the terrace of the Algiers Residency, eating boiled eggs. Nothing any longer had the effect of surprise... That night was the worst we spent throughout the whole trip. Barbara and I were quartered in what passed as an Officers' Club. Our room, we found, had already been taken over...by bedbugs. Sleep was impossible. The meal beforehand, however, made up for much. We had been taken to dine at some delicious Algerian haunt. Our escorts (one of whom was Serge Obolensky) were full of charm and desert war stories. Fortunately, the RAF were able to repair our plane, a considerable comfort as we flew over many plane wrecks.

In sharp contrast, the England we found ourselves flying over next afternoon was shrouded in snow. It lay spread-eagled below us, as we flew east from Land's End, like some sleeping Nordic beast. We seemed to have been at war forever.

The Big Three – Stalin, Roosevelt and Churchill – at the Tehran Conference in 1943

38

All the signs were, though, that the long-awaited moment would arrive next spring. Gladwyn's much updated plans for his long-projected "Four Power Plan" were now coming in to their own. I had had precious little to do as his secretary while away, but now all the stops were out, Agnes welcomed us back with customary shyness, and thereafter the office became a battlefield.

The date of our marriage had been fixed for the following April, and early in the New Year, I sadly said good-bye to Gladwyn, in order to begin preparations. Agnes gradually gained courage in coping with her impossible boss, and the following autumn Gladwyn took her with him to San Francisco where the United Nations was born. Tragically she was killed on the way home together with other Foreign Office members when the plane they were in crashed, in the Californian Mountains.

John and I married on April 15th and the honeymoon was spent on Exmoor, in what should have been a quiet little hamlet with a gushing stream full of enticing trout. John was to teach me fishing, but alas all we ever caught were American cans and empty cigarette packets. We were close to Dunkery Beacon with the Moor stretching out in all directions around us. Unfortunately, the American army was limbering up for D-Day and the noise of firing pursued us everywhere we went. John's new partner in life seemed unable to stand on her feet – indeed, was perpetually lying in the bracken – trained as she was to fall flat at the sound of London explosions. (John appeared unmoved.) What was worse, the American Tiger tanks, on whose patch we appeared to have landed, hurled their enormous bulk along the Devon lanes, their turreted occupants being roughly on the level with our little hotel bedroom!

No, it could not have been described as the idyllic honeymoon, and it was quite a relief to settle into our own tiny turreted top-floor flat, close to Manchester Square. Following an unbreakable F.O. ruling, whereby no husband and wife were allowed to work under the same roof, I had to leave my job in Gladwyn's department. Instead, John arranged for me to join the small contingent of Free French and their English colleagues working till all hours in preparation for D- Day. This was essentially a military establishment – nearly everyone there dedicated to caring for the agents working with unbelievable courage across the Channel.

Hours at the FFI (Field French Intelligence) tended to be long, and I frequently arrived home later than John. One evening while it was still quite light I could see from our 'eagle's eyrie' a flying bomb heading in our direction. John had his back to me, engrossed in washing up. The 'doodle-bug' (a V.1) cut out just above us and I held my breath. John, however, showed no evidence of having heard anything, continuing to dry our supper plates slowly and methodically. I couldn't bear the waiting and shouted, "John, didn't you hear it?" He turned with total calmness, murmuring, "Yes, that mouse has been squeaking for the last fortnight…" I can see him now – giving a final wipe to the meat plate in his hand!

When D-Day came, on June 6th, the families of those involved all gathered together in the Guards' chapel, not more than a hundred yards away from our office, to pray for the safe return of sons and fathers. We ourselves became aware that a flying bomb or "doodle bug" was heading in our direction. In the event, it slid past us almost touching our windows. Meanwhile uniformed bodies hurled themselves under tables and waited. We were extraordinarily lucky to be so narrowly missed. But in the meantime the bomb made a direct hit on the Guards' Chapel, killing, agonisingly, the families gathered there in prayer. On the personal side, I miscarried soon afterwards, losing our first baby – a little boy – and in the event, spent only a short time with the Free French. Perhaps this was just as well, as I had not had an opportunity to build up a relationship with those more than gallant French agents, whose well-being was so closely linked with my colleagues.

Finally, VE Day arrived and a huge crowd collected in Piccadilly. We should like them have been exhilarated and in a mood to celebrate. In fact, we had been so close to the unfolding events at the end of the war that we had discounted the possibility of not finally achieving peace. Now that it had arrived, our task was to reinforce it. John's subsequent appointments were directed at this task.

Thanks to frequent visits from flying bombs (both V.1s and V.2s), our attic flat had an almost uninterrupted view of the area between Oxford Street and Marylebone Road, and apart from the hideous smell of the porter's cats in the basement where all too frequently we would spend the night, we were happy and engrossed in the exciting arrival of Nevil, our first (surviving) small son. We knew, however, that we were due to be posted and that Paris was our likely destination.

Our wedding in 1942

The British Embassy in Paris

CHAPTER FIVE – *A Diplomat's Wife*

"Delighted to hear you are succeeding me here. Come over and see if you 'd like to take our flat." This message, couched in typical FO 'cher Collègue' language, was from Peter Scarlett, outgoing Head of Chancery in Paris.

So there we were – dressed in our English couponed clothes: I in new tweed suit from our little man in Knightsbridge – complete with hideous hat acquired nearly two years before, for our wedding. We caught an early morning plane, and clocked into the Castiglione Hotel, before taxi-ing to the 16-ième arondissement and the Scarletts' flat.

This flat was on the edge of the Bois de Bologne in a building known as the Maison Suez. It had been occupied by senior Gestapo officials during the war, and was equipped with furniture annexed from 'enemies of the Reich'. Everything was now the property of the Ville de Paris, and during our stay there we received more than one couple searching for the (very) special furniture they had lost. Our ambassador at Paris at that time was Duff Cooper and his wife was the well known and remarkable Diana Cooper. Our tour round our new flat, conducted by the Scarletts, was interrupted by a call, apparently for me, from the Embassy. Diana Cooper's voice said she understood that John and I were in Paris, and she wondered if we would join her and Duff (Cooper) for lunch at the Embassy… "Déjeuner en toute intimité of course."

Earlier I had told John with amazing self-confidence that he need not worry about my French – that at school we were forbidden to speak anything else, and so on… quelle déception!

An hour later we were ascending the long grand staircase at the British Embassy and, to our surprise, were met by our hostess half way up. This was a shock. The beautiful and famous Diana Cooper was dressed in the latest Parisian fashion, black décolleté dress and huge black hat.

Lunch, "en toute intimité", consisted of eight people, among whom were Jean Cocteau, Christian Bérard and an English author, Anthony Thorne (unknown to us). Conversation was of an intellectuality I had never met before. Jean Cocteau paralysed me, my French emerged from my mouth like a bevy of newly hatched toads, and the beautiful Diana, as was her wont, looked through and beyond me with devastating blue eyes. Back at our hotel, I remember throwing myself on the bed in tears of fury… "If this goes on, John, I'll leave you."

In the end, we spent four years in Paris. Two years were in the Embassy where John was "Head of Chancery". This involved being in charge of administration, and also embraced staff welfare, where I felt I could contribute something to help John. However, this welfare rôle resulted in us having few working contacts with the French and, in turn, meant that we had less social contact than we had expected. The Embassy, of course, had originally been the home of Pauline Borghesi, Napoleon's sister. A few years after our time there, Gladwyn, my former boss, became Ambassador in Paris; and Cynthia, his wife, subsequently wrote an excellent history of the House, which is more Palace than House.

I had arrived in Paris with Nevil and Nannie at the end of August, 1946. The impact of this arrival had been magical. Chestnuts were already bronzed in Ave. Henri Martin. Children were scampering happily. John had been on his own for over a month, and had brilliantly engaged cook and parlour maid in readiness for our arrival. The flat was large, airy and shabby. Nevil was seven months old, and I had brought Nannie with me to look after him. I had come to know her as an auxiliary nurse at East Grinstead hospital. She was extremely plain, fervently Baptist and the soul of slapdash good nature. She was regarded generally as a one-off and subsequently accepted as such when, in due course, John and I moved on, and she entered another family.

Our household, as usual, took time to settle down. Rose, the cook, was a culinary jewel from la Vendée, of whom we became very fond. She was somewhat over fifty, and when things (i.e. cooking) became too much for her, she would lament, " Mais je suis vieille, Madame. Vous ne comprenez pas."

Thanks to Rose, we kept up quite a fair standard of entertaining, despite food shortages and my own initial shortcomings as Maitresse de Maison. The eighteenth century schoolroom round table we had chosen to bring with us lived up to expectations where informality amongst out guests was concerned.

Our second surviving son, David, was born in Paris, at the hospital given to the British Colony by Richard Hertford (alias Wallace). I was ex-officio Chairman of the Hospital Ladies' Linen Committee, and at the time when I became pregnant, several young mothers had died during childbirth in the maternity ward, which was known to be extremely unhygienic. In fact, in those days – quite contrary to present conditions – French medical care was somewhat suspect. Although Lord Hertford (Richard Wallace of the Wallace Collection) had given the Hospital to the British Community, its terms of reference were unclear; sometimes it was described as a Hospital and sometimes as a Hospice for the British Community. This consisted largely of Nannies and Governesses, most of whom had been interned at Besançon during the war. The result, of course, was a cross between an undistinguished hospital and a work-house. The building had formerly been part of a religious order, and consisted of gloomy (not to speak of dirty) gothic architecture. It was made very clear that it was incumbent on me to reverse a situation whereby all maternity patients were now flocking to the American Hospital.

There was just time to change things, and I managed to keep my impending motherhood a total secret for the first three months. Before the end of that time, I was able to give a Ball in aid of the Maternity Ward at the Hertford British Hospital. I am happy to say that the Ball was a great success – enabling me to give birth to our second son, David, six weeks later, in a smart and totally renovated ward. I believe I was among its first patients!

(I thought I had managed to conceal completely my rising terror at this child-birth, but I had not reckoned on the relaxing effect of gas, and it later transpired that I had given the whole show away in the presence of a pained house-surgeon!)

Most of us wives in the Embassy were in our late twenties. We arrived from England in couponed clothes, and the impact of French Couture hit us fair and square. A certain milliner – Mme Robert of the rue du Colisée – transformed us all. We went mad about her hats, generally choosing the most daringly unsuitable. (I remember adorning myself with a red toque with cock feathers cradling my chin.) When the Minister for War, Mr. Bellingham, visited Paris with his German-born wife, an unforgettable lunch party was given for Mrs Bellingham by Hilda Salisbury-Jones. She was the charming and forceful wife of our Military Attaché, General Sir Guido Salisbury-Jones. We were all sporting our recently acquired creations, and Hilda was unable to take her eyes off the guest-of-honour, who was dressed in severe grey, with a soft grey felt hat. At last, out it came:

"Dear Mrs Bellingham, you really must let me introduce you to my hatter."

"Thank you, Mrs Salisbury-Jones, but I am quite happy with my hat."

Lunch continued, and Hilda was not to be restrained. Her offer was repeated at least twice, and as we all politely thanked our hostess before departing, she announced, "I am now going to take Mrs Bellingham to see Mme Robert and…"(beaming at us all)…"don't you think it's an excellent idea?" Poor Mrs Bellingham looked as if she was on her way to the electric chair, but she was swept out of the door by an ebullient Hilda.

Meeting Hilda somewhere that evening, I asked how the millinery visit had gone. Hilda was looking mystified. "My dear," she exclaimed, "yes, she did buy a hat – and just imagine, my dear. She chose one exactly similar to the one she had on. Too extraordinary, my dear."

Guido and Hilda Salisbury-Jones retired soon after this. Their departure was regretted by the French, for whom Guido was 'the very perfect model of a modern

Major-General' and had endeared himself in particular to all his French colleagues by a remarkable biography of General de Lattre de Tassigny. They settled at Hambledon in Hampshire, where Guido proceeded to lay out elaborate plans for a vineyard, taking his gardener to France to help in the meticulous choice of vine roots.

In due course the moment arrived for the first Hambledon vendange, and Guido invited a close friend from Paris for the occasion. Solemnly the first glass was drawn and, just as solemnly, handed to the honoured guest. There was a prolonged silence, and eventually Guido, unable to bear the suspense any longer, asked; "Et bien, mon ami?" The bon vivant from Paris cleared his throat; "Et bien, mon vieux, le vin c'est comme les femmes! Quelquefois on a besoin d'une grande dame… Et quelquefois? Quelquefois on a besoin d'une petite dame – toute frivole." ("Well, old chap, wine is like women – sometimes one needs a great lady and sometimes a beguiling little flirt.") Fortunately, through the following years the Hambledon wine showed progressive improvement and indeed acquired a certain distinction. Alas, Guido and Hilda are no longer with us and the vineyard is now only a memory.

At the Paris Peace Conference, the French President gave a Ball at the Elysée. This was a wonderful occasion for dressing up, and some of us went to a very chic hairdresser, emerging afterwards almost unrecognisably sophisticated. The belle of the Embassy wives was, I well remember, Hazel Richards, who wore strings of pearls wound elegantly through her hair. We were all rather proud of ourselves.

It must be said that Paris was hardly the easiest first posting for a diplomatic wife. Parisian bourgeousie, infallibly dressed in pitchy black, gave inexperienced newcomers a hard time. In this immediate post-war period, accusations of collaboration were constantly used in attempts to malign the character of one's enemies. Younger Embassy staff were often taken aside by artificially concerned French men and women (mostly women). "Vous savez, Madame, votre ambassadeur et sa femme recoivent frequemment Le Duc de Bot. Ils sont sûrement au courant du fait que… (You know, Madame, your ambassador and his wife frequently entertain the Duke of B…They do realise that…" And, on another tack, "Vous êtes sensible, sans doute, Madame, qu'il existe un ménage à trois chez votre ambassadeur?…" ("You are no doubt aware, Madame, that a threesome exists in your ambassador's home?) Immature though I still was on arrival in Paris, I rapidly began to learn something of life.

Towards the end of their 'reign', the Coopers gave an unforgettably splendid 'Soirée'. Pauline Borghesi's magnificent house fairly blazed with candle-lit candelabra, and the women guests vied with each other in dazzling creations made at the Grands

Couturiers. There was only one slip, but it was an unfortunate one. One of the de Grammont family – close friends of Duff and Diana – arrived wearing the twin of the dress ordered by Diana from Molyneux for this special occasion. Quel drame!

In 1948, the Coopers retired, moving down the road to the rue de Lille. They were succeeded by Sir Oliver and Lady Harvey. You could hardly have found a couple more different from their predecessors, and the flamboyance of the recent past vanished in favour of modesty and quiet, discreet intelligence. Oliver had acquired, over the years, a small and distinguished collection of French paintings which he took pleasure in showing to French guests. Maudie was of Isle of Man origin, and full of her own warmth of personality. I remember her being somewhat nonplussed at the first dinner they gave for the French Foreign Minister, when with Gallic gallantry he informed her that "her smile stretched from Paris to London." "Do I really have such a large mouth?" she wondered. Sadly, the relationship which developed between the Coopers and the Harveys was very painful for the latter couple. Nancy Mitford described the situation in fairly accurate detail in her novel "Don't Tell Alfred".

It must have been about the time of the Peace Conference when the legendary Ernie Bevin (British Labour Foreign Minister) and his wife Flo arrived for the weekend at the Faubourg St. Honoré, and Maudie Harvey needed help with hospitality. We arranged to give them dinner on the Sunday night- and pulled out all the stops because Ernie was almost worshipped by the Foreign Office. We even engaged a white-gloved, positively aristocratic butler to stand by the lift and press the button on the second floor the moment the British Foreign Minister arrived. Unfortunately, Monsieur Roueff, a very high-level French financier, lived on the 6th floor. He was dining out, and he pressed his lift button at precisely the moment when Ernie eased himself into the lift downstairs. (He was a big man.) There followed a good ten minutes when we thought we had lost Ernie. Monsieur Roueff at first summoned him up to the 6th floor, where he was extremely surprised to see Ernie, whom he knew, ensconced in the lift. Before proper niceties could be exchanged, our old butler pushed the 2nd floor bell. And so it went on. A purple-faced and irate Ernie eventually stepped into our drawing room, where John had wisely prepared a huge whisky for him. Gradually the great man relaxed – and then…

It was not to be our evening. A family of middle-eastern teenagers living behind the paper-thin walls of our flat began their nightly practice of Chopin's polonaises. Ernie was just warming up on a subject dear to his heart when Chopin drowned him. At this moment, our ancient hired butler threw open the doors and announced dinner. Outrage hung frostily in the air and followed us into the dining-room.

The first course had been carefully chosen for Flo, who had previously asked Maudie Harvey what a truffle was. John was desperately trying to keep things under control. He turned to Flo to inform her that she was eating truffles in her scrambled eggs. To his horror, he saw that she had finished, and there was a row of small black objects carefully positioned by her on the side of her plate. (Needless to say, truffles had never before come into our, or it seems their lives. They had, of course, cost a fortune.)

In 1948 General Marshall set out his design for post war economic recovery. As a result, the OEEC (Organisation for European Economic Co operation) was set up. Its headquarters were just opposite our flat at the Château de la Muette. As a result of his economic experience, John was appointed as one of three deputy-heads of the British Delegation to the new organisation under the leadership of Sir Edward Hall-Patch, from the Treasury.

Before we left Paris, there was an exciting visit from Princess Elizabeth and the Duke of Edinburgh. Oliver and Maudie, ever thoughtful for their staff, arranged for senior members to share the planning of royal visits to nearby places of interest. It fell to us to escort them to Versailles. The Princess was pregnant at the time, and as I was in the same boat, in the elaborate dress-rehearsal which preceded the visit, I was used as the guinea-pig for climbing unusually taxing staircases, and so on. There was considerable anxiety about the whole visit, as a group of terrorists had just tried to blow up our Embassy in Rome, and the French police were on top alert. The Versailles visit went off without major incident though I blotted my copybook forever with the then Princess by wearing a huge (very Parisian) navy hat, which successfully hid the royal presence from her cheering crowds.

Our colleagues taking the Royal couple round Fountainebleau, however, had a rather too interesting experience at the restaurant in the forest where lunch was laid on afterwards. Like ourselves, they had had their earlier rehearsal, and had explained to the patron that the Royal pair wished to arrive at the back of his popular restaurant without running the gauntlet of inquisitive guests. Unfortunately this had slipped the mind of the restaurateur – and when Hazel and Brooks arrived rather ahead of the Royal Rolls, they found the entire back courtyard jam-packed by the vehicles of hungry guests. Panic ensued and the cars were smartly removed by their owners – all except one, which was unclaimed. By this time the restaurant patron was apoplectic, and shortly before the arrival of the Rolls, he flung himself on the car and effectively forced it open. Inexorably it began moving forward, gathered speed and dashed into the small lily pond in front of the back entrance – thereby flooding the courtyard. At this moment, as might be guessed, the Rolls turned the corner.

Our delegation to the OEEC was headed by Sir Edmund Hall-Patch – a distinguished economist and bachelor. His three deputies were Sir Hugh Ellis-Rees from the Treasury, John my husband, Foreign Office, and Sir Eric Roll – subsequently Lord Roll of the Board of Trade. Eileen Ellis-Rees I remember as a woman who always lived quietly – a gentle woman who, when Hugh became head of our UK delegation, was consumed with shyness. The men were all top economists, and I suppose there was inevitably a degree of interdepartmental rivalry. But from the start, OEEC promised well.

At the start of a new decade, news came through that John had been appointed to New York as ambassador so we left Paris in 1950 – taking a short leave in England before setting off for the U.N in New York. We divided up the mountains of luggage – and while John drove to Southampton in our new car, stuffed to the roof, I took the train from Waterloo station with the rest of our belongings. The train was about to start when there was frantic knocking on the double doors and a little old lady could be seen desperately trying to force her way in. I helped her, gave her my seat, stowed her luggage and never thought about the episode again.

I joined John on the Southampton docks and we settled into our cabin on the Queen Mary, one of the two Cunard sister ships that plied the Atlantic and the pride of Great Britain. Our ship towered above the offices on the quay as we arrived at the station. Ocean travel in those days was a huge adventure and I felt excited to wake up and find ourselves surrounded by the magnificent vista of the Atlantic. Next morning we were walking on deck, eyes fixed on the seascape all around us, when we were approached by a very tall man with a fragile white-haired lady hanging on his arm. "I must tell you," he addressed himself to John, "how immensely grateful we are to your wife for looking after Mrs. Andrew Mellon so wonderfully yesterday on the train. My name is Lauder Greenway, President of the Metropolitan Opera…and by the way, do join us tonight at the Captain's table."

This, as a beginning to our life in New York was, to say the least, the stuff of fairytales. It had been magical enough just to arrive and stand on the Queen Mary, awed by the glittering skyline of the city. The impact of the New York skyline, however you arrive, is electric, and as the Queen Mary edged its way towards the jetty so far below, the effect on the newcomer is overwhelming. Lined up at extraordinary heights and angles, those apparently Martian skyscrapers pressurise you from every direction. The final touch would be to discover that John's new office was situated on the 34th floor of the Empire State Building, which was in those days the tallest building in the world.

On arrival, our new friends threw a party to greet us – and thereafter there were always seats for us in someone's box during the two years we were in New York. All ill-

Nevil (left) with me and David

Me on the Queen Mary, with New York
skyline behind (Photo by John)

deserved but what a difference it made to our musical,
as well as social, life.

We lived at first in a converted Vanderbilt
garage at Great Neck, Long Island. The UN was
about to be transferred to New York, where the new
building, resembling a huge inverted matchbox, was
nearing completion. Our garage must have held at
least five Cadillacs, and a roof loft conversion made
it just possible for a family of two adults, two very

The Queen Mary

small boys, their Nanny and an extremely unpleasant Dutch cook to squeeze in. Our first
three months there were largely uneventful but peaceful. Two events stand out in my mind
in this connection. One was a totally impromptu lunch we laid on at two hours' notice
when the Russian delegate Malik was proving totally intransigent at a Security Council
meeting within the UN Assembly, and John thought a meal 'en famille' might calm him
down (it did).

The second event was a particularly virulent hurricane, which struck as John was
leaving for Poughkeepsie to spend the night with Eleanor Roosevelt and make a relevant
speech. When he eventually arrived at a lightless, chaotic Poughkeepsie, his speech had
been cancelled. However, it was quite an experience to be the guest of Eleanor Roosevelt.

Luckily for me, our landlord – a charming little fellow living on the southern shore
of Long Island – turned up to see if all was well. He spent the night with us, arriving

with a formidable axe, which, he explained, would be useful if we had to cut our way out. Fortunately we managed not to use it – but in the morning fourteen trees were down all around us.

Before Christmas we moved to a large, light flat on the corner of 72nd Street and Lexington Ave, NY. This was relatively close to the new UN building, which enormously simplified matters. Central Park, also, was not too far away for the children although quite a trek with a pushchair. As I have mentioned, John's office was on the 34th floor of the Empire State Building. The views were magnificent and our children loved an excuse to visit him!

Social life fairly buzzed with activity and, wonderfully, our new operatic friends made sure that we had regular invitations to one or other of their boxes. This was hard on John as he was all too rarely able to be there. But on the other hand, it was a wonderful and educative experience which I will never forget.

Just before Christmas I took the children to see Father Christmas at Wanamaker's Downtown. He lifted David (then 18 months old) onto his knee, and began questioning Nevil – looking increasingly puzzled. "Say, what kinda dialect is this?" he called to me. I explained that we were newcomers in NY and that we were English. "Don't worry, he said," consolingly. "They'll soon lose it!"

Those days with the UN were full of excitement – and faith in the future. Shortly before we arrived, President Truman had taken the momentous decision to commit the US to war with North Korea and most of the UN had followed suit. (This was the same President who had, five years previously, dropped bombs on Hiroshima and Nagasaki, and thus precipitated the end of World War II). The Russian emissaries, Vychinski and Malik, however, seized every opportunity to accuse UN members of war-mongering. Television had just come into its own and the head of the British delegation, Gladwyn Jebb, took part in nationwide programmes in which, as far as the American public was concerned, Gladwyn emerged as St. George, and one or other of the Russians as particularly nasty dragons. (This was a new role for Gladwyn, my former boss,.and he took to it with self-satisfied relish.) There was a general feeling, in fact, that right was seen to be done and in fact Gladwyn – architect of the UN – was at the helm.

New York itself was, of course, heady stuff. At that time optimism was in the very air you breathed and as someone remarked, "There's not a street sweeper who doesn't believe that, given half a chance, he can become President one day." Language, too, as we have seen above, could be a problem, language and enunciation. I remember going, for the first time, to buy liver at the local butchers. I was dazzled by men with enormous knives, wearing

John speaking in New York

John and me on the top of the
New York Port Authority building

white straw hats. One of them looked up and said; "whatyer want, ma'am?" At which I lost my head and answered; "I want some liver." "Whose liver? Mine?" was the retort. And then, the hunt for a saucepan! It had never occurred to me that there were two ways of saying "aluminium". And the one I knew mystified any hardware salesman.

How much easier, though, for us than for immigrants from Central Europe! Our daily cleaner, Maria, had recently arrived from Hungary and her English was naturally monosyllabic. Each day she attended "New Citizens'" classes – learning to swear allegiance to the American flag as a priority, and slowly, slowly adding a word or two to her vocabulary. Maria was no linguist, but it must in any case have been juggler's work, caring for a clutch of small children, struggling along with her husband to keep a roof over their heads and managing to prove to the world that they were becoming good American citizens.

Soon after we arrived in New York I was asked to a lunchtime seminar given by Adelaide Stedman – a well known political lecturer, whom we had met through Christian Scientist colleagues. To my horror, I was introduced as the wife of an Englishman, attached to the British Delegation, at the UN and was asked to give a talk on my government's views on the war in Korea. It was a miserable occasion, which of course taught me an invaluable lesson – the necessity of learning to assemble what views one had coherently, and present them in public.

I will never forget the sequel. Each night I was involved with John in UN affairs of one kind or another – and this precluded any kind of evening class. It proved almost equally impossible to find a daytime course, though I eventually ended up in a large West-Side New York hotel, as part of a course run by Mrs. Dale Carnegie – wife of Dale Carnegie whose book "How to Make Friends and Influence People" was a "must" for keen young business men. His wife ran a less intellectual and more general course for women designed, I seem to remember, to teach students how to be a joy in the home and how to be articulate in public.

That first night there must have been over sixty people gathered in a large dusty hall and it took little time for me to discover that every one of them (excluding, I hoped, myself) suffered from some impediment – twitching nose, trembling chin, etc. A professor from Columbia University marched in, and we were made to go up, six by six, to a platform. The professor then asked simple questions of each victim – getting them to give their name, address, and reason for their being with us. On the whole it worked. A bright, black, young laundress from Brooklyn had no problems. On the other hand, a (hitherto confident but brash) secretary from mid-town N.Y. responded to the professor's questions by clutching her nether parts and yelling; "You scare the pants off me."

Right at the end, he addressed himself to a very tall girl (she must have been 6ft) with long dangling arms. "May I have your name please?" No response, and she stared ahead as if petrified! Eventually, with huge difficulty, he elicited her name, and then, with equal hard work, made her whisper where she came from. This caused quite a sensation, as it was Alaska. "Really, Mrs. Hilton, how interesting! And which airline did you use to get here? Transair? United Airlines? American Airlines? …" Complete silence and her mouth started to work. Eventually, in the hoarsest whisper, she managed; "I piloted myself!" She never came again.

Madam von B. from the Dutch Delegation came up to me at a reception a few days later. She was large, handsome and commanding. "I hear you are attending public speaking classes. I should like to come along with you as I am becoming rusty – not being a delegate myself on this occasion. Let me know the time and date of your next lecture." Rather like the girl from Alaska, I opened my mouth in an attempt to warn her off. It was quite useless. There were only about thirty survivors at the next meeting and among them I saw my friend, the cheerful black laundress from Brooklyn. I was embarrassed, though. Very. Madam von B. had turned up wearing a very dressy black outfit with a huge hat. The professor came in fussily and explained that this time we had to stand up one by one and describe in three minutes the most dramatic event we had ever experienced. Off we went with accounts of situations in our lives which had particularly impressed us.

I cannot remember what my little laundress described, but probably something like the ceiling falling down on her as she worked in her Brooklyn basement. The professor was offering a silver pen as a prize, and, yes, you've guessed it, Madam von B. won hands down with her little talk entitled "The day I visited Mussolini".

John and I decided to see something of the Western States – feeling we might never have another chance. (How wrong we were!) We left our children with obliging friends holidaying in Cape Cod with their own small fry, and, with endless help from friends, planned a trip which took us ultimately to the Grand Teton mountains in Wyoming. There we stayed on a ranch with the writer Struthers Burt and his wife. To get there we went by train to Saltlake City, where we picked up a car and drove southwards to the north side of the Grand Canyon. The Mormon state of Utah was in itself a source of much interest to us, as we had read extensively about the Mormons and their origins, and were intrigued to hear from the National Park official who took care of us at the North Rim that polygamy was still practised in remote corners of Utah.

The log cabin we occupied at the North Rim was the stuff of dreams. Nowadays when, through the Internet, you can "drop in" on places of the kind quite casually, it is hard to realize the thrill of finding ourselves in a Fennymore Cooper setting – (almost, anyway.) In fact even today I can smell the resin and feel the comfort of that little cabin with its welcoming log fire.

As for the Grand Canyon, there we were at a height of 6,000ft, gazing down through the millennia – strata upon strata – all this dusty pre-history contrasting astonishingly

The Grand Tetons, Wyoming, USA (Photo by John)

54

with Utah's two spectacular National Parks – Bryce Canyon and Zion. Bryce, with its mix of absurdly-balanced minarets, provided a huge contrast with Zion, where a huge and dominant rock exuded an extraordinary sense of mystery. In both parks, the soil was the colour of marmalade, giving the impression of ancient surrealism.

And before leaving Utah, it is worth recording that, in subsequent years, we were to come across the remarkable dedication of young Mormon missionaries. Under State law, every one of them must serve a year, after finishing at school, as a young proselytiser in "foreign parts". I have seen the effect produced by two young men on an Italian household in Geneva. The family man was deeply Catholic. And yet these youthful missionaries had them on their knees. To those who have followed the origins of Joseph Smith's Faith, this provides food for thought.

Crossing the Hoover dam we made our way in withering heat to Las Vegas where we had to board a train at midnight for San Francisco. John was carrying his fishing rods in long aluminium cases, and we became aware that we were being followed as we sought our seats. Eventually a polite official asked us to unload the aluminium cases and the penny dropped! John had become a suspect for gun-running – a new role for him!

Struthers Burt, our host on the ranch near Jackson Hole in Wyoming was a splendid raconteur, and introduced us wonderfully to our surroundings. A small man, his appearance hid the fact that he was actually extremely tough, and a sensitive writer to boot. A 'western' saddle took some mastering – but all in all it would be hard to beat the sense of freedom we encountered on the ranch.

Bryce Canyon in Utah, USA.(Photo by John)

Family at Bromley c. 1951

CHAPTER SIX – *West of Suez*

We said goodbye to America the following year (1952) with some sadness- never thinking we would be returning only three years later. John was recalled to be Economic Under-Secretary in the Foreign Office, and we moved into a newly-completed block of flats at the top of Exhibition Road, South Kensington, Princes Gate Court. Those were good days in London. Suddenly we seemed to know a whirl of people of all nationalities who regularly squashed themselves into our small drawing-room for drinks, canapés and exchange of ideas as friends. This was a situation which unquestionably paid off – and was of course of immense value for John.

At the same time, our sons were growing up fast and, at six, Nevil was enrolled at Hill House, one of the more successful pre-prep schools in London. It was owned and run by Col. Townsend, who was never referred to by his real name and answered only to "Sir". We parents thought this amusing, of course. "Sir" was a keen sportsman, and I well remember that at our interviews with him he was totally uninterested in hearing about Nevil's precosity in the Classics and constantly turned the conversation to football and cricket. (A little later, Hill House was chosen to be the 'pre-prep' for Prince Charles.)

David was still just too small for pre-prep schooling, so a mother's help became essential, and a large humourless Dutch girl came to live with us. One day a friend living in the same block, to whom I had recommended the agency she came from, kindly phoned to say that in answer to her advertisement our Dutch girl had presented herself on their doorstep. This had surprised us – and when John returned from work we asked Ans to join us in the drawing-room. When asked if she were unhappy with us, she flushed purple and in an outraged voice said; "It is David. He bites." and she lifted her skirt to show us a small but distinct bite on her leg. Now David, who was three, was of course a small Holy Terror. His parents, however, had never been aware that he bit. Poor Ans!

But yes, those were good years in London – Theatres, Christopher Fry's "The Lady's not for Burning", John Osborne's "Look back in Anger", etc etc. And then the opera – our first visit to Glyndebourne. Unforgettable among these was, of course, the day of the Coronation in June, 1953. We were up at 3 am. I found it very strange to be dressing in the middle of the night, wrapping layers of white gauze round myself like a sort of Cinderella, and even putting a little crown on my head. As for John, he was dressed up in full diplomatic uniform – navy blue covered with gold braid, with a sword fastened to his belt.

When we stepped outside, the streets at first seemed rather empty, but the nearer we came to Westminster Abbey the more crowded they became until people were standing sometimes six to eight deep. Many of the crowd had been waiting for up to three days and nights. Sadly it was drizzling in a very English way. All those waiting people had macs and rugs but by 5am nevertheless, they were slowly getting completely soaked.

When we reached Parliament Square we heard a newspaper boy (we used to have them in London then) crying, "Everest conquered!" Everybody cheered their heads off. The news that our own British team (led by Edmund Hillary from New Zealand) had just reached the top of the highest mountain in the world was given just in time for the Coronation and seemed a wonderful omen.

We made our way into the Abbey where John had a special rôle

The Coronation in Westminster Abbey, 1953

to play. He was a Silver Stick, which meant that he had a silver and blue coronation stick with a gold crown at the end and a spike. He had to keep the passages clear as people began arriving. Naturally, because I was of no importance, I had a seat behind a pillar in the third row on the left as you faced the altar. The seats near me began filling up with Peeresses (mostly wives of the Lords). They wore plum-coloured velvet and ermine hats shaped rather like a crown. By this time it was about 8am and people were becoming hungry. Suddenly, out of the peeresses' hats came small packs of sandwiches. Those hats must have held a lot, as all through the ceremony boiled sweets seemed to pop out. (One of John's jobs was to pick up sweet papers with the point of his stick to make sure nothing spoilt the wonderful main aisle. Another was to look after a marvellous lady – the Queen of the Tonga islands in the Pacific Ocean. She was the largest, fattest, jolliest Queen you could imagine and she just loved driving in the coach they gave her – waving to all the watching crowd).

Meanwhile the Royal procession was forming outside Buckingham Palace. Slowly, foreign kings and queens in their carriages began moving down the Mall, across St. James's

Park and arriving at the huge West Door of the Abbey. Finally, with a fanfare of trumpets, Princess Elizabeth arrived, together with all her attendants. There she was- Princess only for another half hour before leaving the Abbey as Queen Elizabeth 2nd of Great Britain. She was splendidly dressed in white and gold. Of course, as I was sitting behind a pillar, I couldn't see very much and missed much of the splendour though I managed to stand up at the moment of the crowning and I shall always remember the Crown – laden with jewels and immensely heavy even for the Archbishop of Canterbury as he held it before placing it on her head. She looked almost crushed by it – and suddenly you realised how desperately young she was to carry such terrific responsibilities.

Among many new friends was Thelma de Chair, Somerset de Chair's legal wife. She had been made a life-tenant of Blickling Hall in Norfolk by the National Trust – and we spent an unforgettable weekend there. Thelma was an ardent Christian Scientist, who had been monstrously treated by her husband and persisted in loving him through thick and thin.

Also staying at Blickling were two well-known National Trust executives who were in the neighbourhood to investigate strange occurrences in a nearby Elizabethan house. In the course of restorations, I seem to remember that the walled-up head of a child had been found.

When I was about ten, my brother and I were taken to Blickling by our aunt and mother. Youthful as we were, we were overwhelmed by the beauty of the house and grounds – not to mention the fact that our aunt hinted under her breath that the house was heavily haunted. Although we were both accustomed to members of our mama's family being obsessed with ghosts, the episode had stuck in my mind.

After dinner, where we were well lubricated, our National Trust fellow-guests began a discussion on ghosts they had encountered in the line of duty. We later made our way to our bedroom. ("I've put you in the Chinese room, Mavis. Mostly Chinese Chippendale, but there are some lovely things there".)

Ready for bed, John went out like a light and, after glancing round nervously, I attempted to do likewise. However, for some unknown reason, my spouse chose that night to try out a series of new snores. They were fairly spectacular and bore resemblance to what I imagine a banshee must sound like. I was paralysed with fear and slept not a wink. Brilliant sunshine met us in the morning and at breakfast, I overheard John telling Thelma with satisfaction that it must have been the best night's sleep he'd had in many moons.

Two years passed and our boys were growing. We had a splendid holiday with them on the Norwegian fjords – and Nevil, at the age of ten, managed an exciting climb/walk

Nevil crossing a glacial
torrent in Norway

John on a fjord in Norway in the late 1950s

to the top of Europe's largest glacier above the North Fjord. There were endless walking goals to achieve and masses of wild raspberries to refresh us – providing we reached them before the goats.

John was Chairman of the Anglo-Norwegian Economic Committee, timed to take place at Midsummer and involving one half day's meeting in Oslo. We stayed with Michael and Esther Wright at our Embassy. Michael was a fisherman, as was John, and for two midsummers running, we ended up staying with the Malteruds. Otto Malterud was commercial minister at the Norwegian Embassy in London. He owned a tiny island off the tip of Christiansand. Otto epitomised the best in Norwegians and was a splendid host. Those were two memorable, although rather alcoholic visits! There was a bracing breeze – powerfully impregnated with fish – and miraculously, the sun shone on each occasion.

On our second visit, thanks to the hospitality of a timber-merchant friend of Otto's on the mainland, John caught a medium-sized salmon. The time of our visit was drawing to a close and John was due to fly on to Stockholm for a meeting. I was to catch the midnight Fred Olsen ship at Christiansand and I agreed to add the salmon to my luggage. It was one of the stormiest nights I have ever experienced and when the ship eventually fought its way down the Oslo/Christiansand channel, I thankfully handed over John's salmon to the purser for safe-keeping.

Next morning, feeling more dead than alive, we made our way to the London train at Newcastle. Thankfully, I found an empty carriage and hurled the salmon (admirably wrapped in layers of the London Times) into the luggage-rack. In due course, the carriage filled up with Danish missionaries – all impeccably dressed in grey – and as the train began to move southwards, I found myself acting as an unofficial guide to this well-behaved group. ("We are now passing York", and so on.) Suddenly, the small, neatly dressed lady opposite me clutched her head and said, very positively, "Sumsin iz dripping." It was. I watched in horror as slow, measured drops fell from the newspaper package above her, through her innocent grey hair and then remorselessly on to that Copenhagen tailored suit. I also heard my shaken voice begging her to come down the corridor where, in an empty toilet, I would be able to sponge it all away. Obediently, as if in a dream, she rose to her feet and followed me. All loos were locked and remained so throughout our journey to London. When I attempted to explain and express my regret to the entire carriage there was total silence. These people, it seemed to indicate, were resigned to persecution.

Back at Prince's Gate Court again I set about preparing the dinner party which we were giving the following night. John was due home in the morning and his salmon was to have been the pièce de résistance. It was clear, however, as something more akin to porridge than salmon emerged from the Times that salmon mousse should be the order of the day – and I'm relieved to recall that it was outstandingly successful.

Those three years in London turned me into a cook, I'm glad to say – and not before time. In spite of endless comings and goings, domestic life, involving two tumultuous small boys, pre-schools, schools and piano lessons had to be dealt with. I remember one night, when I was running horribly late for yet another dinner we were giving. The boys were behaving abominably in their nursery – paying no attention to their mama's instructions to (in modern parlance) "cool it". The nursery looked down into a well, and as I eventually charged into the room, brandishing my frying pan in fury, I became aware of numerous eyes following my every movement – and waited for the door-bell to ring.

In 1955 John was asked by Roger Sherfield (then still Roger Makins) to join him as his No.2 in Washington. Roger was an ideal choice as our Ambassador there. Married to Alice Davis, with resultant excellent American connections, he had been posted in Washington during the war and, as they say, knew everybody. A towering man (both physically and mentally) he later went on to be, first, Head of the Cabinet Office, and then, Leader of the Atomic Energy Commission. He was an influential member of All Souls, and seemed to be involved in every possible intellectual and economic enterprise.

Our Embassy in Washington was high-powered, with three major sections: political, economic and commercial. John was the British Minister, a title that non-Washington socialites found confusing. On one occasion, in a small town in Maryland, we were at a reception given, I have a feeling, by the Daughters of the American Revolution. One chatty lady approached me and asked what John did for a profession. I told her he was the British Minister, and she commented keenly, "How interesting, my dear! What denomination is he?" When I explained that he was No. 2 in our Embassy, she was clearly disappointed.

The Embassy is an impressive Lutyens building on Massachusetts Avenue. Through the years it has infuriated countless Ambassadors' wives, who have struggled to make it into a welcoming home – a goal which has rarely been achieved. John and I were resident in another house owned by the British, on Kalorama Road. This had originally belonged to the Makins, during the war. It was next door to an exotic family of Irish-Americans from Texas. George McGhee had recently returned from Turkey, where he had been U.S. Ambassador. His wife was charming and certainly prolific. (They had six children ranging from five to eighteen years old.)

From the word 'go' we seemed linked with the McGhees. Our six-year-old son immediately identified a soul-mate in the penultimate McGhee child. They played on the garden wall and became a disruptive force which became part of the scene. The day after we arrived, when I was frantically unpacking, there was a peremptory ring at the front door. A very small girl was standing there with a dog, which she introduced as 'Fanshaw – our half-basset'. She marched in as though owning the place – though Fanshaw initially left half of himself behind. "I'm Cecilia McGhee," the diminutive creature announced; "and Fanshaw wishes to go to the bathroom." Having satisfied herself about the new neighbours, she then retired.

Prolific they were indeed, our next-door neighbours! Fanshaw (who of course turned out to be female) constantly produced enormous litters of pups. More than once I caught her desperately hunting for food in our rubbish bins. (The Irish-minded charming masters must have found it hard to remember that there was a canine mouth to feed, on top of satisfying rumbustuous, hungry McGhees.)

One morning, 'Ceil' (George's wife) called me in some excitement – asking John and me to lunch that day. "Our favourite Prince is coming," she announced proudly. John was already booked for lunch, so I went on my own. There were eight of us and the Prince turned out to be Prince Bernhardt, from whom George had difficulty in removing his eyes. Chicken in some succulent sauce was served and we settled down to enjoy it. I also settled down to enjoy my neighbour, a new lawyer friend from down the road. Engaged as I was in conversation with him, it was a little time before I turned my attention back to my food. Suddenly a very heavy flump descended on my knees and, as I turned quickly, I was just in time to see a huge tongue, unmistakably Fanshaw's, whip round my plate, neatly vacuuming all traces of chicken. As I pushed Fanshaw down, I looked up at my host on my left, and burst out, "Did you see that, George?" George was smiling benignly and gazing as if mesmerised at Prince Bernhardt. Seeing my somewhat astonished face, he murmured, "You had finished, hadn't you?" At least it was flattering that Fanshaw had recognised a friend!

George had married the daughter of a well-known geologist and was heavily into oil extraction in Texas. He was also available for 'special duties' when called on by the President, and was frequently absent from Washington. One day I asked him how he ever managed to direct his oil enterprises in such a hectic life. We happened to be in his study, and he pointed to a map on the desk, showing a particular project.

"It's so simple, Mavis. I just lift the phone, look at the map, pinpoint it and say; 'Drill here, boys...' and they do!"

John had, from time to time, to take up speaking engagements – some on the West Coast. When I discovered that my fare would be paid if I went with him and talked to local women's groups, I determined to join 'The Capitol Speakers' Club' – a very reputable school for public speaking, run by a Mrs Provensen. This was the best thing I ever did. The 'club' was a Godsend to newly-arrived Congressional wives who for the most part came from small unsophisticated communities across the vast country which is America. I can't honestly say that the subject matter was particularly inspiring – and I only attended half the course. But it was a wonderful way to get to know Congress – which we managed to do in under two years. Also, the door was open for me to travel with John.

Social life in Washington was at a peak – nightly political dinners in different Embassies and Washingtonian homes – and so many drinks parties that we used to divide up the list between us. And then there were splendid evenings at the Waltz Club, and so on. Where dinners were concerned, John felt cheated as, according to protocol, I had, of course, the most important Congressional male guest on my right, while he had a tongue-tied and nervous wife next to him. "Such a waste," he murmured.

Meanwhile, events were developing worryingly in the Middle East. Anthony Eden – delicate and ambivalent – was proving to be the reverse of the dependable British leader Britain so much needed at this time. Months of negotiations had been taking place between London and Washington on how to curb or dispose of Nasser, the Egyptian leader. When finally proposals for funding the High Aswan Dam fell through, Nasser was thwarted and responded by nationalising the Suez Canal.

Eden immediately advocated the use of military force to recover the canal. President Eisenhower and Dulles, his Secretary of State, though favourably disposed towards Britain – it was after all a 'Special Relationship' – proposed an international conference and the avoidance of the use of force. It was clear to the Embassy in Washington that Eden had completely misread the American position, believing that the US government would not oppose unilateral military action by Britain. Eden failed to understand that Congress, who would have had to be recalled in the summer recess, would never agree to an intervention in advance of the imminent US elections. Moreover, public opinion was opposed to any military strike. Dulles needed time to get past the elections and to educate public opinion if any military action could be envisaged. It was for this reason that Dulles, with the support of his President, at this stage suggested setting up a canal users' association (SCUA) and instigating economic measures against Egypt. Incredibly our British Prime Minister never properly understood that SCUA was in essence a device by Dulles to buy time until after the presidential elections, i.e. he was doing his best to support Eden.

Paying scant attention to the advice of military and diplomatic leaders, however, not to mention specific warnings from Eisenhower, Eden went ahead with plans to occupy the Suez Canal in a tripartite collusion with France and Israel. The diplomatic bomb that exploded in Washington as a result was a surprise to no one on the spot. But the decision to occupy the territory was a total surprise to the Americans and British in Washington alike. Before the attack on Egypt Roger Makins was recalled to the United Kingdom to become Head of the Treasury. As we have seen, Roger and his American wife, Alice, had provided a reassuring and popular bridge through the years, and their departure was deeply regretted – particularly as Roger's successor-to-be, Harold Caccia, was to arrive after a gap of some weeks. There seems little doubt that the gap before the appointment of the new Ambassador at such a crucial moment was entirely deliberate on Britain's part. Eden and his collaborators determined not to instruct their emissaries in the relevant parts of the world and particularly not in Washington. Thus it was that neither Roger Makins, while he was still there, nor my husband had any forewarning of the intention to occupy the canal. But it was John who, as Chargé d'Affaires, had to explain the British position to an exasperated President and Secretary of State..

My husband, at an extremely tense moment, found himself moving constantly between Eisenhower's office and that of Dulles. I have a vivid memory of a lunch party – arranged weeks beforehand – for the Bishop of Washington and his wife. The meal was conspicuous for the absence of the host as, arriving from talks with the President, he had no sooner greeted his guests apologetically than he was summoned to the Secretary of State's office. The Bishop's wife wrote a charming letter afterwards, in which she mentioned 'British phlegm'.

At this moment, Charlotte (Lady Bonham Carter) turned up in Washington. Her reputation for 'never missing a trick' brought her first to New York, where her friend Bob Dixon, head of the British delegation to the United Nations, was attempting to hold the UK front. She then moved on to Washington, where another 'dear friend' i.e. John, was in charge. Sadly, fond though he was of her, this diplomatic venture was entirely unproductive – much to her disappointment. (It was not at all clear how her intervention could have been productive but her intent was definitely benevolent).

These were difficult days for those representing the UK – not to mention the French – whose minister was also left holding the fort. Fortunately for John, he knew the State Department terrain quite thoroughly and was able to escape by back routes while his unfortunate French colleague was obliged to face the press each time he stepped out of the elevator.

Our new ambassador, Sir Harold Caccia, arrived a couple of weeks or so later. The Anglo-American atmosphere was still tense and, as John could not spare the time for a flight to New York, I was sent to represent him. It is the only time I saw Harold 'edgy'. He showered tense questions at me, most of which I was ill-equipped to answer – though at least I could give him an idea of the atmosphere he was about to enter.

In the meantime, the international situation had eased slightly, though matters were further complicated by Russia's invasion of Hungary and, as I have indicated, the astonishing way in which Eden had withheld all information about his plans from all his representatives around the world. We had friends in the CIA, and knew of their involvement in the whole Hungarian situation. All seemed to be going well, until the Suez debacle came along, distorting the whole picture. For weeks afterwards, we, the British, hitherto their warm friends, were held responsible for the complications which ensued. Very gradually the atmosphere began to clear and Washington, always prone to volatility, began to settle down. The 'Special Relationship' between Britain and the United States, however, was slow in returning.

We had many and varied visitors, among whom were Selwyn Lloyd, Chancellor of the Exchequer, Denis Laskey (his PA), and Sir John Cockcroft, head of the Atomic Energy Authority.

Once Harold Caccia was properly installed as Ambassador, John began a series of visits to the American West, in an endeavour to explain our conduct in the Middle East. (Nobody, however, was able to understand Eden's extraordinary secrecy.) Fortunately for me, I was allowed to accompany John in order to speak to Women's Clubs and so on. Life then became normalised and with cherry blossom and a burgeoning Washington

Spring, morale rose.

One summer's day in Washington before I left with the children for England, to escape the Washington heat – it must have been in 1957 – I returned from the day out to Kalorama Road in Washington to find an empty house. In our shared study there was a note on my desk. It said laconically, "They've made a lady of you at last!" And it was like this, in his inimitable way, that John told me he had been made a knight – in the order of St Michael and St George (KCMG), the order of which he was already a Member. The following Spring, we received invitations to attend the ceremony at Buckingham Palace and, to our great satisfaction, John's father, recently widowed, was included. It was a great day for Granddad, and he savoured every moment and I have to admit that I also was overcome with pride. After all it was generally believed that the conferral of a knighthood on John at a relatively young age while he was still Number Two in Washington formally recognised how well he had handled an exceptionally difficult diplomatic crisis.

The news of John's knighthood was naturally most exciting. There followed a very active and very hot summer, and I then left with David to join my mother in Sussex. She had been ill for a long time and our visit was important to her.

I was in her lovely small garden after dinner one night when I saw her looking for me. "Quick!" she called, "It's John." Those were in the days when there were few private international calls and I was astonished, and said so. My mother, though, had always been a bit clairvoyante, and told me calmly that she knew what it was about. She was right. We were being recalled from Washington, at three weeks' notice, instead of staying on for a further three years, as expected. Poor John! I was furious at being moved so summarily. Before leaving Washington to come to England I had been made President of the Capital Speakers' Club, besides other things, and had been looking forward to the challenge. John, however, was exhausted by his recent experiences and did not deserve a disgruntled wife.

No sooner were we back in London than he vanished on the new job which was to assist Reggie Maudling in establishing a Free Trade Area in Europe. I managed to find a questionable ground floor and basement flat at the bottom of Gloucester Road. There was something about the atmosphere of the place which I found disconcerting. The porter, who said he was leaving the next day, regaled me with the chilling sex-life of the flat's former owner: "The first night, it was. Rushed 'er to 'ospital but it was too late…" Long pause. "And then 'e married again. Must of been a night or two afterwards! Ambulance came but she died soon after…! An' then 'e marries again…" I controlled myself. "And then what happened?" "Oh! I dunno, never 'eard. An' then 'e left the country…"

Next morning I met our porter on the stairs and told him I had passed a poor night after our previous conversation. He looked at me pityingly and said, "You ain't 'eard the 'alf of it." Eventually he mentioned that his predecessor had hanged himself on the downstairs door which communicated with his and our flat. Nevertheless, I must have left my mark on him, because when we were leaving he commented to my elder son, "She's a woman and an 'alf, your mother". Yes, Wetherby Place, it is hard to forget you.

It was after Christmas, and I was with the children in Sussex with my mother. Such had been the shortness of time for our removal from Washington to London that we had great difficulty in finding a school for David (then eight and a half years old). When it was becoming a losing battle, the inept young headmaster of his brother's prep school came forward with an apparently firm offer. ("If we can't fit him in elsewhere we'll put him in the bath!") This was one of many problems at the time and, to my shame, I gave in.

The phone rang early one morning at my mother's house at Upper Hartfield. It was the porter from Wetherby Place. ("Think the burglars has been, Lady C. There's a basement window open, and a gin bottle and towel by the bathroom basin!" I asked him to check on a drawer in our bedroom. (Until then I had never locked anything.) "See if there are any empty jewel cases." He rang me back to say that there were three large empty jewel cases but 'everything very tidy.' I drove to London with the boys to meet the police – only to be told that they had come and gone, saying they could find no trace of any attempted burglary. While I was in discussion with the porter, my eight-year-old David had lifted up the large counterpane over our bed. There were at least sixty little empty jewel boxes hidden beneath it.

John was home briefly at that point and due to leave for Paris next day. We were dining out that night with a colleague in Regent's Park. During the course of dinner our burglary was inevitably discussed. "Be careful!" an ominous voice announced across the dinner table. "Burglars always come back, in the event of failure to find a particular "piece" they are looking for."

John left early next morning, and when Detective Smith arrived to take stock of the situation, I asked him whether there was any truth in what I had heard. He confirmed that this was so – and I then pointed out that not only would I be alone that night but I had no 'phone or other means of communication in my room. Detective Smith appeared uninterested, so I asked what would happen if I woke in the night to find the burglars back on their treasure hunt. Detective Smith looked at me coldly. "Well, they could of course kill you," he remarked helpfully – and then doubled up with laughter.

Soon after this I ran into Iris Hayter in Sloane Street. She was surprised to see me,

John with David and Nevil and Elsa

thinking we were still in Washington. Fury and frustration burst out of me as I described the way the Foreign Office treated their wives… "Squeezing you like lemons at one moment, and the next, folding you neatly in tissue-paper at the back of the housekeeper's cupboard."

It is to this hysterical outcry that I owe the next move in my life. Iris, whose husband was at that time Ambassador in Moscow, was longing to get rid of a job which she did not need. ISS (International Social Service) was, for the United Kingdom, a relatively new charity – but in fact had come into being in 1921, as an endeavour to cope with refugees from eastern Europe converging on Holland and Belgium in a desperate effort to reach the United States.

It was not until the 1950s that another charity in the United Kingdom – The Family Welfare Service – saw in the whole exercise an opportunity to unite Family Welfare Service in Europe – and indeed globally as its ultimate aim.

The Family Welfare Service, under the leadership of Kathleen Luce, had the blessing of the Foreign Office, who saw to it that an experienced FO wife should always be on its board. As I said, Iris saw her chance to unload this on a colleague and I rose perfectly to the bait. To my dismay, I found myself a member of the Appeals Committee, a job for which I felt myself totally unsuited, given the fact that the management of finance was not one of my accomplishments.

I represented the Charity at a depressing 'United Charities' sale at the Dorchester. This had a certain snob value but made very little money, and at the end of that experience, we decided to invest in our own Spring Fair the following year, and to 'go it alone' at the Chenil Galleries in Chelsea.

Four or five of our 'diplomatic' friends ran stalls representing their Countries, and at the end of the day we had made £500, which seemed riches to us. John and I were posted to Sweden the following year, and I handed over the chairmanship to a colleague. This in fact became the pattern of the Fair as it is today. Thanks to all our diplomatic friends, and the fact that the event is a wonderful way of bringing the world together, what began as a small triumph of £500 is today an enormous achievement, bringing in on average £140,000 in a day and an evening. I had hoped to shed ISS before we left for Sweden, but things turned out otherwise.

At the Old Mill, Selborne, in the 1960s

CHAPTER SEVEN – *Home and Abroad*

In the spring of 1958 my mother died. John had lost his mother the year before, and realising, with the prospect of another impending move, the need to establish another base for ourselves in England, we began searching in the West Sussex/ East Hampshire area. Being very different people, we entertained very different ideas on the subject – until one Saturday evening, tired and frustrated, we wound our way down a twisting drive in Selborne, a little Hampshire village, and discovered the Old Mill at the bottom. Now John, as I have already mentioned, was a keen fisherman and the sound of a trickling stream appealed highly to him while exciting in me easily-aroused romantic feelings. The mill itself was in a run-down state, and the miller's house – well, let us say that here was a small dwelling which provided the sharpest, yes, almost too sharp a contrast to the "official " dwellings we were accustomed to inhabiting abroad. Instantly we turned to each other with the words, "This is IT!" And it was… together with the still abiding aura of Gilbert White.

Meanwhile, Margaret, the nannie and companion of my youth, and her husband, Keith (elderly and frail) came up from Devon for my mother's funeral in East Sussex, breaking the journey at the Swan Hotel in Alton. At dinner they were joined by a garrulous but charming fellow guest. It turned out that she was Irish (very) and had bred Shetland ponies at the Old Mill in the recent past. Before parting, she asked Keith and Margaret to convey a message to us – the new owners. "Tell them, my dears, that it was I who built the high retaining wall behind the house. The fact was that one winter's night there was a violent storm, and the hill began to break up. And out of the hill came human bones – arms, legs and others. Well, rather than have those damned archaeologists interfering, I quickly got hold of my friend the builder, and made him brick them all up again. Yes, do tell your friends, my dears! They lie very close to the outside larder's window."

I received this news as we were about to have dinner in our London flat and immediately told John that nothing on earth would make me move into the Mill, and the sooner we phoned the owner, cancelling the verbal agreement, the better. Meanwhile, John had ascertained that the old lady was the mother of a colleague of his at the Treasury. He phoned him and, as I sat and bit my nails, I heard a one-sided conversation: "Hello! Is that you, Hugh? Hugh, my wife and I are about to buy a house which belonged to your mother in Selborne…yes, that's it – the Old Mill. The fact is, Hugh, that friends of ours have just met her by chance and she told them a strange story… something about the hill behind the Mill falling down in a thunderstorm – yes, yes. So you do remember it? Well, your mother described the disgorging of many bones… Yes, exactly. Well, they were undoubtedly cows' bones, weren't they? So, many thanks, Hugh. I'm so grateful to you." And he hung up with extreme speed.

From the word "go" our Old Mill was a total success. Our first family home was excitingly different from anything we had known before – and although the rebuilding required made life uncomfortable for many months, it was enormously worthwhile. In their holidays, the boys worked hard in the garden, and at weekends we would feed and water obliging friends who helped us transform a makeshift swimming pool fed by the stream into – well, something a little less amateur. My mother had been a besotted gardener and I must often have been a great disappointment to her because I used to lap up the finished product but remained totally uninterested where creativity was concerned.

Now, however, there was a new element in our lives – a garden which was ours and which required our careful attention. I brought over a garden designer from Hillier's to help design what inevitably had to be a water garden. I remember Mr Dallymore – yes, I know that was his name – standing silent and motionless above the stream. I longed to know his thoughts and eventually broke in on his reveries with; "So what do you think, Mr Dallymore?" Whereupon he turned and said, "Great possibilities, Mrs Coulson. " And that was all.

Anyway, we loved our stream-motivated garden, and made the most of it as far as we could. In fact, it was endlessly alluring, and very much a family project. However, no sooner had we established its broad lines than the local sewage company decided to run a supplementary branch-line through the very middle. This was a nasty shock – though the company responsible could not have been more helpful in repairing what damage could be undone.

John's appointment as our Ambassador to Sweden in 1960, unexpected though it was at the time, was a happy one. The Swedes liked him and had, they felt, chosen him. He arrived on May 9th and the Svenskadagbladet carried a large picture of him subtitled, "Sir John Kommen", (Sir John is coming) in which he looks shyly pleased at their welcome. Standing beside him is a somewhat surprised wife in a questionable hat! Our old Norwegian friend, Otto Malterud, of course speedily put the cat among the pigeons by sending a telegram en clair to the British Embassy. It read, "Best of luck in the Wrong Country!" (But that, amongst Scandinavians, was, one supposes, predictable.)

The day we left Selborne, spring was bursting around us, and the garden alive with little happenings. Quite a shock then to arrive in Stockholm in early May and find black skeletoned trees and an apparent deadness wherever you looked. Our new Swedish friends assured us that within a week or ten days there would be a complete change and sure enough, quite suddenly, bluebells began to appear as you looked at them and the Northern Spring began exploding. Our new home, the British Embassy, was beautifully situated at the edge of a lake – an extension of the nearby Baltic. The King of Sweden and his first wife, Margaretta, had been close friends of the then British Ambassador and had helped "landscape" a small garden for them just above the water's edge. This was as original as it was successful for it developed into a rockery-cum-herbacious border! Both Gustavus VI's wives were English and it seemed a very happy arrangement.

The King's heir, married to Princess Sybilla, a German, was tragically killed in an accident at the end of the last war. When John and I were in Sweden, the present King, Carl Gustav, then a boy in his teens, and his three sisters (one of whom, Princess Margaretta, married an Englishman, called Ambler) lived with their mother at the Palace. Prince Bertil, the future King's uncle, was Regent-in-waiting, and had an amusing little partner, also English. The old King was an astonishingly erudite man where the arts were concerned – indeed, where nearly everything was concerned. He was quite charming and with great deference I called him my "Royal Pin-up".

I remember an evening when the Anglo-Swedish Society arranged a lecture to be followed by a formal dinner. We were spread out around tables of eight, and on account of John's position, I found myself sitting on the left of the King – a great honour. Something went very wrong with the catering, and neither food nor drink were produced, apart from a large glass of water for the King. We all began to be tormented with thirst, and eventually I nerved myself to say, "Sire, would you allow me to drink your water?" H.M. looked interested, and replied, " Certainly, Lady C. Have you got hiccups?" I shook my head, and he looked crestfallen. "But what a pity, Lady C," he murmured, "I know a wonderful cure for hiccups… You go behind the lady and lift her up by the ears. Whereupon I instantly said, "Sire! I do have hiccups." at which he replied, "Oh no, Lady C! What would people think?"

Apart from the King's wit, it was an appallingly-served meal. (Most unSwedish!) At the end, coffee cups were brought in and left empty. At this point the King did his best to cheer things up. "We'll have a game of Jenkins' Up," he suggested. "Has anyone got a crown?" This was too much for my friend Malin Ihre. "Tell him," she hissed, "he has!" and having made the point with him, I was extremely glad to see the arrival of the coffee. Oh, a lovely man!

On another occasion two well-known English sculptors arrived in Stockholm to give an exhibition. Armitage and Chadwick were and are remarkable creative artists and the King was apparently anxious to see their work. It was arranged that John, as Ambassador, should open the exhibition and that the King should then accompany each sculptor in a tour of the room. Although I myself was delighted with their work, I knew it was hardly John's 'cup of tea'. However, he made a nice little introductory speech, looked round the room rather sadly (I thought) and announced, " And I now declare the exhibition closed!!" This reduced the King to near-hysterics, which of course did help to promote international goodwill.

Drotthingholm's remarkable – and until shortly before our arrival – hidden small Operatic theatre in the grounds of the Royal Palace at the edge of Stockholm has an intriguing history. This small, lost, eighteenth century gem had been re-discovered shortly before our own arrival in Stockholm.

It was arranged, I suppose about halfway through John's incumbency, that Benjamin Britten, with Peter Pears, should bring over the English Opera company to perform Purcell's "Dido and Aeneas". The theatre was of course the perfect venue. The "intendent"

John in a State Coach going to Present his Letters at the Palace in Stockholm c. 1960

With the King of Sweden, in Stockholm   At the Embassy before leaving for the Palace

of the Palace came to see us to discuss plans for "Dido", and told us the following amazing story. He was an elderly courtier and was making his regular inspection of the palatial property when he happened to see a dangling piece of cord poking out from the front of a small building. Punctiliously, and as part of his job, he seized hold of it and tried to pull it. To his amazement, he felt something like a screen obligingly beginning to advance towards him. He went on tugging, realising that this "screen" had many companions. And thus were revealed, I think, about 40 original eighteenth century Opera screens in, it appears for the most part, excellent condition.

Sweden is almost heartbreakingly beautiful in (to us) late spring. No wonder that the Swedes, emerging from their winter armour, strip off and run for their little red stugas (wooden huts in the forest next to lakes) and beckoning boats. At first, when we arrived, it seemed as if our new Swedish friends gave one look at us and fled. A year later, we began to understand and to respond ourselves to the earth's explosive yielding. No shy appearance here… The real thing is thundering round you. Yes, you feel the whole primeval world is leaping, thrusting –and at last you understand what Strauss was after.

One of our most memorable trips, at midsummer, was a visit to Dalarna – at the heart of Swedish folklore. We stayed with Swedish friends, the Axelsson-Johnsons, in their converted miller's house at Avesta. (Axel Axelsson Johnson was Head of the Axelsson Johnson Steelworks, and had his own shipping line.) There was a pretty oval-shaped drawing-room, and our Brazilian hostess described to me the family's arrival at their new home. As her parents were unpacking, their small daughter, aged about seven, became engrossed in tricyling – ovally. Suddenly she appeared in her mother's bedroom.

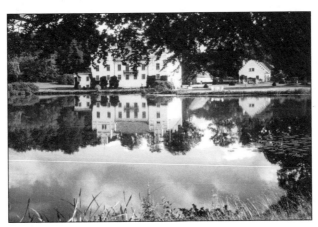

Vanas, a country house in Skorne, where we stayed

"Come quickly, Mama! There's a man sitting in a corner of the sofa. He is holding his head in his hands, and looks very unhappy."

Her mother followed her into the drawing-room and sure enough, there was the man, just as her little daughter had described him. Helena rushed into her husband's study. "Axel," she whispered hoarsely, "come at once! There's a man sitting in the drawing-room and he must be a ghost."

Axel was interrupted in the middle of an important calculation, and was not moved by his wife's information. "Well, shut the door immediately," he said with some annoyance, and continued to add up. When they returned to Stockholm Helena consulted a friend on the subject, who instantly told her what to do when he made his next appearance. Helena followed her instructions implicitly and next time the ghost reappeared at Avesta she spoke loudly and clearly; "Go away at once! This is our house, not yours. GO AWAY! GO AWAY!" Apparently, this treatment worked like a charm and the lugubrious gentleman was never seen again.

There is very little dark in the short Swedish summer nights. We gathered at Avesta that midsummer evening in broad daylight, and by midnight it was twilight and dawn would soon be breaking. The Dalarna fiddlers arrived with folkloric equipment, and we were seated (as became John's ambassadorial title) at the table of old Fru Axelsson Johnson – mother of Axel and a fairly formidable old lady dressed austerely in black.

With John before the opening of Parliament, Stockholm

Leaving the Embassy for the opening of Parliament

76

Dancing began during dinner, and the twenty year old son of great friends of ours presented himself at our table and asked me to dance. Ulf was later on to become Swedish Ambassador to Washington, and thereafter Head of the Swedish Foreign Office, but that night he was just a charmingly polite young man who took me on to the highly polished floor and proceeded to teach me how to "twist". This was distinctly energetic, and in order to stay upright I kicked off my shoes and "fell to it". When he escorted me back to Fru Axelsson Johnson's table, I collapsed happily back in my chair – only to hear the old lady remarking with acidity; "What strange people they accept nowadays in the British Foreign Office!" (This was accompanied by an audible sniff as I hurriedly put on my high-heeled shoes.)

I can remember now, as though gazing into a crystal ball, the following morning's stroll through the Avesta Ironworks and along the river leading to a weir. Sunlight was brilliantly refracted through pine trees and a group of teenage friends (the girls nordically blonde and beautiful) leant on railings above the weir pool. Suddenly they seemed transfixed, as if mesmerised, as they stared into the molten gold below them. Stuff of dreams – ah yes! – a moment out of time. And even now – forty years on – I see those puzzled searching young faces – caught, for a brief moment, in mystery.

Midsummer in the Arctic Circle was, of course, another experience. We had booked into a small, basic hostel on the edge of Lake Torneträst, and the sun blazed relentlessly and scorchingly on and out of the water. We attempted to walk in what was really tundra, and by 11 pm the sun began to make us cross-eyed so we gave in and crawled back to our hotel bedroom. Dawn was now gleaming and with the help of blankets we managed to black out an indecent sun.

Before leaving Sweden we paid another visit to the far north, this time to Kiruna, heart of the iron-ore mining activities. Conditions on this occasion were the antithesis of our midsummer adventure. No light, except a curious sparkling of deep-frozen snow, no noise apart from the rumblings of a vast iron-ore activity. John's friend Arne took us to see an astonishing little art exhibition for which he was responsible. In a cave-like construction were hung the creative paintings of primary school Eskimos, all of them concerned with their winter background of snow, frozen lakes and dramatic looking mountains. He kindly gave me one of these paintings which I treasured. I remember finishing the so-called "day" with reindeer bones from which you sucked the marrow – traditional food for the nomadic Eskimos.

Swedish design was and is of the highest quality. Glass (crystal) and ceramics in our time there were matchless and this reputation for excellence was something shared with "Arabia" in Finland. We were close friends of the Heller family who owned Orrefors.

With our dog, Vasa, on the Embassy veranda in Stockholm

I will never forget descending on the Orrefors factory to see the Lucia "festival" on December 13th. Alas, John was too busy to leave Stockholm, but a close friend, Lia von Sydow, took his place at the last moment, and for eight hours we journeyed through enchanted snow forests.

The rail-track to the Swedish South ran through Orrefors property, and it was "gratifying", as my old aunt would have said, to have our train stopped specifically for Lia and myself. We spent that night in the manager's house, and were woken at 4 am by the tramp, tramp of feet on snow, as the factory's staff converged on glowing glass ovens. Every Swede knows the legend of Santa Lucia, or rather, I should say, legends, for there are many. Selma Lagerlöf's story appeals to me most, and is worth a brief mention (told in Appendix 2).

Meanwhile, the little factory band began tuning up and Santa Lucia (always the blondest and youngest girl present) was helped to adjust her crown of lighted candles, while her attendants – traditionally a small clown and a fairy – lined up behind her, accompanied by the classic tune of "Santa Lucia" (no Swedish folksong this, but for some odd reason a Neopolitan fisherman's song.). As the small procession moved between the roaring glass ovens, Lucia proffered cakes to each team of workers, and the heat of the ovens was diffused and extended to the entire gathering of happy Swedes.

During our time in Stockholm, the annually-awarded Nobel prizes were distributed, with a particularly important award given to an Anglo-American couple, Francis Crick of Cambridge and a seventeen-year-old American, James Watson, from Stanford University. Both of them had worked together on unravelling the genetic mysteries of the "double helix". Young Watson, at the end of a long, champagne-flowing ceremony, was escorted to the Grand Hotel, where he collapsed on his bed and knew no more. Not for long, however. He was awakened from drunken dreams by his bedroom door opening to reveal a beautiful blonde girl with lighted candles on her head advancing towards his bed. Watson, we are told, was convinced that he had died and was about to meet his Maker. He passed out completely.

Lia and I were escorted round the ovens, meeting the artists and wondering at their astonishing glass-blowing achievements. Later, we were taken into the pine forest to meet one of Orrefors's top artists who was housed by the management in a small cottage. I still have the remarkable transparent apple (half a metre high) that I had seen her blow early that morning.

Our journey back to Stockholm was unusual. Our fellow passengers were for the most part commuters returning home for the night, and they bored Lia, who was used to high-life companionship, and indeed was a legend in all five countries where, by chance, we had met previously. Night had fallen and the view from the train window consisted of pines, heavy with snow blankets, dimly lit by the lights from our passing carriages. Suddenly Lia began to sing rousingly. Half the passengers were, or had been, asleep and the air was filled with astonishment mixed with indignation. Lia appeared unconscious of the rising atmosphere of antagonism around her, and continued her programme of unclassifiable music. As a non-Swede, I was consumed with embarrassment. Oh Lia, Lia.

Our last Swedish summer was coloured by the raising of Gustavus Adolphus's flagship from the entrance to Stockholm's harbour. It had been the Vasa's maiden voyage in 1625, at the beginning of the Thirty Years' War, and this had caused considerable excitement as the Swedish army embarked, together with the ship's crew and a substantial group of families to cheer them on their way. The ship was brand new, and the hatches were open, ready for the barrage of fire to be used in the farewell salute to Stockholm. Up until then, the harbour waters had been perfectly calm, and the families were assembling on deck, ready to disembark. At that moment, a freak wind sprang up, with the result that the ship began to list a bit to port and waves began to engulf the hatches open for the salute. (The current theory is that the design of the ship was wrong). As the ship listed to port, the as yet unchained cannons all rolled over to the port side. The ship (named Vasa after the long line of Swedish kings)turned turtle and sank like a stone, with all on board. At that location, Stockholm's outer harbour was immensely deep so all contact with the ship promptly ceased. It wasn't until the early 1960s that a young sailor by the name of Anders Franzen succeeded in pinpointing Vasa – and the long, slow process of bringing her back to the surface was begun! With immense caution, the Swedish Navy began to excavate her, deck by deck, storing each artefact in huge rocky caves in the harbour, where they were immediately plunged into chemically-treated water baths.

In the summer of 1964, this all caused intense interest, and I seemed to be guiding the then so-called "Visitors Firemen" on regular weekend visits to see the Vasa relics. In fact, I fear that the young marine guard with whom I was in such regular contact will never forget me.

It was an exceptionally hot and busy weekend and my three houseguests (consisting of Roger Stevens, a former British Ambassador, with his wife Constance and Ann Dupree – an old and sadly handicapped friend) showed obedient and genuine interest as they toured the many artefacts housed in the momentous pottery-lined containers, impregnated with chemical water.

Roger peered into one of these after we had just been informed that they were of special interest: cannon balls discovered on the main deck! Roger was a tall man and had some difficulty in discovering the treasures before him. He managed, though, to find an appropriate epitaph and "They look rather like large brown potatoes." he murmured. Whereupon I heard my voice say loudly and clearly, "Oh no they don't, Roger. They look exactly like Swedes." And catching the horrified look on my marine's face, I completed the horror by saying, "I do beg your pardon. But you see, in England we eat Swedes!"

One of our holidays in Sweden was
a skiing trip to Dalarna

SUMMER NIGHT: SWEDEN

Oh night of mother-of-pearl,
Nostalgic night!
The enigmatic lake
Is gleaming white.
Across the meadow mists
Are stringing sights…
Slowly, the elk emerge –
A sea-bird cries

And in the cool, white night,
Caressed by flowers,
The little old wood house
Ignores the hours –
Dreaming, in pallid rooms,
Of crowded years –
Man's Vulnerability,
Euphoria, tears…

Oh night of mother-of-pearl,
Nostalgic night!
The birch is stretching limbs
In growing light.
A nightingale high in
The lilac spray,
Heralds immortally
The earthly day.

Romantic portrait of me by a Hungarian artist in Stockholm in the early 1960s

CHAPTER EIGHT – *Southwards to Geneva*

John returned from Sweden, in the summer of 1963 to become "Chief Clerk" (a much more senior position than it sounds) at the Foreign Office at a time when the Foreign Office and the Commonwealth Office were about to be amalgamated. This was a delicate operation –involving as it did personalities, pride of history and so on. As John's wife, I was made chairman of the F.S.W.A. (Foreign Service Wives' Association) and Lady Garner was my opposite number of a rival European Economic Group, representing the Commonwealth wives. In the event, her husband Sir Joseph Garner (Jo) was made head of the two offices. It must be said that I have few memories of this period – though I do remember, that Peggy Garner and I spent an earnest morning choosing designs for the housing of diplomatic families in the about-to-be established new capital of Pakistan – Islamabad.

It must have been about this time that the loneliness of "Second Eleven" foreign diplomatic wives came to the attention of the FSWA. It was recognised that wives of Ambassadors and their "number twos" were well cared for by Government hospitality and organisations particularly concerned with the individual countries, while further down the ladder, "foreign" wives received little or no attention and were clearly powerless to help themselves. Lady Harrison (Mimi) and I called a meeting of Foreign Service wives to discuss the problem, and much to our surprise we found that some of the victims (so to speak) were actually in our midst, in the form of the considerable number of foreign wives of British diplomats who actually complained of their own loneliness! As a result of a subsequent meeting at Lancaster House, the wives of the more junior foreign diplomats were asked to come forward, giving details of where they lived and whether they needed help. Maps of central London and the Home Counties were spread out on the floor of a large flat near Victoria Station. Letters which had come in offering help from English diplomatic wives were carefully studied as to their location, making it possible to establish little groups in and around London, the would-be hostesses being encouraged to bring in their local friends – wives of doctors, lawyers and so on. Thus we set up "Diplomatic Neighbours" in about 1964. Somewhat to our astonishment it immediately flourished and continues to do so today.

In the winter of 1958, when General de Gaulle was still denying the possibility of the United Kingdom joining the Common Market, John, together with Reggie Maudling, later Home Secretary, had been one of those invited to an international think-tank meeting in Saltsjöbaden, Sweden, to discuss the setting up of a rival economic European group. EFTA (the European Free Trade Association), as it was called, was subsequently set up in 1960 and comprised the United Kingdom, Sweden, Norway, Denmark, Austria, Portugal, Finland, Switzerland and, later on, Iceland and others. Frank Figgures, a brilliant and volatile member of the United Kingdom's Treasury, was chosen to be the first Secretary-General of the new organisation, to be situated in Geneva.

A year or two after John and I left Sweden, Frank had a severe heart attack, perhaps exacerbated by the shock of finding that his own country (the United Kingdom) was imposing a 15% surcharge on all foreign goods coming into the United Kingdom. (This made complete nonsense of the elaborate "Free Trade" arrangements made between all EFTA countries). Frank was invalided home, but not before John and I had flown out to take over their house in Geneva, as, to our extreme embarrassment, the other EFTA member countries had insisted that John take Frank's place.

This decision meant cancelling the "agreement" we already had with the Spanish government whereby John was to become our Ambassador in Madrid. However, in Whitehall it was considered of crucial importance in the circumstances, and all our plans were revised. The prospect was daunting but, as so frequently happens, this new posting proved to be full of interest – not to mention the exciting new experience of finding ourselves in the centre of Europe.

Frank and his Viennese wife, Aileen, had been living in an impressive 17th century house belonging to the Ville de Genève (ie the State). It had belonged to a distinguished Genevois family, the Candolles, and Roger de Candolle, the then surviving member of

Chateau de Chillon on
Lake Geneva, c. 1970

View of Mt. Blanc from the Saleve,
south east of Geneva

the family, could boast one of the foremost 18th Century European naturalists as his ancestor – Auguste Pyramus de Candolle. Roger's house had a magnificent double verandah, and on rare but wonderful days we had a brief view of Mont Blanc on the eastern horizon.

Unfortunately, the Ville de Geneve had been in the habit of letting it when and where they could – and the Russian delegation had been the Figgures' predecessors. The furniture their Government had commissioned from the Ville was atrocious (acres of red carpet). Nothing could improve its appearance and, although John and I had brought some of our own furniture, it was impossible to distract attention from what was hideously bureaucratic taste. What was more, there was less than a year to run before the lease of the de Candolle house would be up.

Here it is important to say that EFTA had introduced a totally new element into Genevan and indeed Swiss life. This was actually the first time the Swiss had belonged to an international organisation of this kind and they regarded EFTA almost with affection. Before we left England we were warned about the coldness of the Genevois, and how difficult it was to make friends within a community determined to preserve its identity against a tidal wave of ever-increasing international organisations. It appeared, indeed, that the Genevois had intermarried for centuries and this had produced a society exceptionally hard to penetrate. How totally wrong, in the case of EFTA, this proved to be.

What a welcome we all received! John and I imported, together with our Swedish colleagues, "The Dancing Habit" after so-called official dinners, and when I return to Geneva, as I do quite often, there are many nostalgic exchanges about the old days! Because, alas, life has reverted to its old seriousness. And then for us, of course, there was the excitement of living in the centre of Europe, the ability to cross the French border as many as four or five times in the afternoon and the romance of the encircling, snow-beckoning mountains!

Once in six months the EFTA Council met in one of the member countries. This of course helped the organisation to know and understand each other's problems, where collaboration was concerned and was full of fun and interest. Britain's Labour Foreign Minister at that time, George Brown, was the Head of the United Kingdom delegation, and we were always anxious to know whether he was drinking or not drinking. The gloom of course was great when conditions were "dry" and I well remember a Town Hall Banquet in Bergen when George was seated between the ample, folkloric figure of the Norwegian Lady Mayoress on one side and his least favourite Central European EFTA delegate on the other. As they were short of a woman at the High Table I was placed between the President of the Swiss Confederation and the Finnish Foreign Minister. Seating otherwise followed the usual pattern, with all other delegates seated at tables placed

John and I arriving at the Mansion House in London
for a banquet in honour of EFTA in the late 1960s

INTERNATIONAL CONFERENCE: GENEVA: MAY

If it were not for the blackbird by the lake
(The silver lake which gleams between the mountains).
If it were not for the willows weeping low
(The willows opening shyly in soft spreading rain),
If it were not for the purpose which binds us
(Binds and cements us all, the more the challenge) –
This constant buzzing of well intentioned thought
Would be an agony.

at right angles to the High Table. Lia von Sydow, who had been with me on the Orrefors visit – the new wife of the head of the Swedish Delegation and a notable joker – was seated not far away from us. Suddenly a paper dart fell into the pea soup which was at that moment being carefully served. The President of the Swiss Confederation helpfully pulled it out. When it had been safely landed, Herr Schaffner solemnly read out the message

John shaking hands with the President of Finland in Parliament, Helsinki

written on it. "HELP!" it said in large letters, "George Brown must be rescued immediately." Herr Schaffner and I looked nervously along the High Table past the enormous embroidered bosom of the Lady Mayoress to where George Brown sat scowling in front of an empty glass, aware that much laughter was emanating from our end of the table. Herr Schaffner, who was a peaceful man, murmured, "Something must be done." Whereupon he again peered over the mountain of satiny material, cleared his throat and said, "Mr Brown, you know Lady EFTA, don't you?" George Brown replied freezingly, "I do" and turned his back. This was too much for me, as I had never met him before – nor was my name Lady EFTA. "No, no, Mr Brown, " I called out. "Of course I'm not Lady EFTA and this is the first time..." George's huge bushy eyebrows vanished into his hair and ostentatiously he again turned his back on me.

Well, he got his own back on me next day at our official drinks party on a small mountain-side. I spotted an old friend (the Norwegian delegate to EFTA) talking to someone invisible. No sooner had he seen me than he pulled me round to face George Brown, who put his hand behind his back.

From the very beginning we met with extraordinary friendship in Geneva and, in the course of time, the doors of the Vieille Ville occupied by the old families began to open. The lesson I had learnt in Sweden – that you must never expect anyone to make the first move in a social relationship – now proved as helpful here as it had been there. All our EFTA group slipped easily into Geneva life, and one friendship led to another. Soon after we arrived we met Olivier and Francine Long. (Olivier became Director-General of GATT in due course, though for a time he was in the Swiss delegation to EFTA and became Swiss Ambassador in London.) Francine and I have been close friends ever since.

The Longs introduced us to Geneva's exclusive small library, "La Societé de Lecture". This occupies a lovely 17th century house in the Grand' Rue. As you step over its threshold, the centuries 'telescope' and you slip backwards, backwards into a thriving late-medieval fortified town, besieged by the Duke of Savoy, and resisting with heroic patriotism – as described in the story of La Mère Marmite and her lethal casseroles of soup which she hurled at every Savoyan soldier who breached the battlements.

History seeps through every crack in La Vieille Ville and old Genevois still tend to conduct their business lives, though with less circumspection as the new century rolls on, behind huge grey gates. Genevois officials, however, were of immense help to EFTA proceedings and firm friendships were made between foreign delegates and their hosts.

As mentioned, John and I soon initiated the after-dinner dancing habit in Geneva. Pale and overworked, Swiss bankers took cautiously to such frivolity at the day's close (one telling me with a heavy sigh that he couldn't bear, while changing for dinner, to see his pyjamas beckoning to him from the bed).

At the end of the first year we moved from Chateau Lullin to a very attractive manoir just outside Geneva, above the Rhône. Previously, we had agreed to rent a friend's house on the edge of Lac Léman. Tragically, however, he drowned in the lake, close to the landing-steps and I fear nothing could induce me to move there. Poor John! He had the tough task of persuading the apparently unyielding Swiss lawyers administering the property to allow us to renege on our arrangement. ("C'est ma femme, vous comprenez, monsieur. Elle est tellement sensible…") It was an enormous relief to escape from that commitment – and fortunately soon afterwards John found himself sitting next to the friendly wife of a Swiss banker who assured him that they had many houses in the family and would be delighted to put one of them at our disposal. Not only was she as good as her word but, with the enthusiasm of an amateur interior designer, she ransacked the attics of other family houses in order to provide us with furnishing gems and even travelled internationally, purchasing further treasures for the house. Oh yes! We had extraordinary luck and the house at Vernier – 17th century manor on one side and early 19th century farmhouse on the other – proved ideal for entertaining and an intriguing home for the family in the holidays. As well as the occasional glimpse of Mont Blanc on bright, clear days, the garden delighted us with spring-time cherry blossom, and had its own 'terrain de boules'.

Vernier had another occupant beside ourselves, and David complained at breakfast one day of hearing footsteps overhead during the night. "Just mice" I tried to reassure him, whereupon he asserted, "If they were mice, they were wearing boots!" It was about then that we were told by Genevois friends about the 'fouens' (martens) who manage somehow

View of the house and gardens at Vernier

to live comfortably in old period-houses without either being detected or creating noticeable damage. David, however, was unconvinced, and as time went on, I too wondered…

Those were 'pioneering' days in Geneva. To the astonishment of many of its citizens, groups were set up whereby EFTA (and indeed other) 'foreign friends' were drawn into Genevan life. Examples of this were 'le Cercle de la Presse', the 'Ville Rigau' gatherings and, most successful of all from the cultural point of view, Geneviève Peyrot's Art Group. Until the 60s, Genevese youth almost inevitably married each other, and I remember raised eyebrows when the son of one of our banking friends, living in New York, was reported to have taken an attractive Turkish girl as partner. The century was on the move though and suddenly there were Swedes, Austrians, Norwegians and, yes, Britons mixing with the Genevois elite.

John and I had a great love of opera, which we shared with many friends over the years, and Geneva offered many evenings of musical enchantment. A letter arrived from Charlotte Bonham Carter one day, which was couched in the following enthusiastic terms: "Dearest friends!

They tell me that darling Elisabeth (Söderström) is arriving imminently in Geneva to sing the title role in Pushkin's Eugène Onegin. I think my plane arrives in Geneva at about 8 am. I wonder, dear John, if you could arrange for someone to pick me up there?" It was perfectly clear who that someone would be, and John duly timed his 8 am arrival at the airport on the appointed day.

There was, however, no sign whatever of a recently arrived flight or of our guest in the (then) dusty little airport. John was finally ready to give up the search when he decided on one last foray behind one more pile of luggage. And there he found a small, crumpled heap, which rose to explain that actually her plane had arrived at 2am, but of course she would not think of disturbing John at such an hour…so she had simply had a long, delightful sleep on an airport bench.

We took the chance Geneva afforded us to travel widely during school holidays with our two sons and this afforded us

Elizabeth Söderström

89

Looking down the Grand Canal, Venice, towards the Salute

Palazzo Polignac on Venice's Grand Canal, where we stayed with the Decazes

some memorable experiences of how Europeans moved in elite circles of their own. One memorable year we were finishing a family holiday in the Engadine, to the far east of Switzerland. We had been joined recently by Jean and Belle de Noue, French friends since our UN days in New York, where Jean had been 'Chef de Protocol' and my John had been No. 2 in the British delegation. Jean and Belle were childless, but somewhere along the line they had become fond of our two boys. We were packing up to leave Sils Maria when Belle suggested we 'drop in' on her ducal brother and his wife at the Palazzo Polignac on the Grand Canal in Venice. "It will give the boys a chance to see Venice as it should be seen. And after all it is no distance if we take the route we have worked out".

And so it proved. We arrived at the city of the Doges at the height of the August season, when Venice was packed with art worshippers of every kind, and palazzo-crawlers dying to be seen chatting to You-Know-Who…

From the moment we were met at the landing stage by Primo (head of staff in prominent Italian houses), we felt ourselves slipping back in Time. The Piano Nobili, on the first floor, was heavily beautiful and full of treasures, while leading off from it were a number of very small rooms of a "toute intimité" kind. Small they may have been but there were enough of them to cater for any of the visitors who might wish to communicate with one another in closeted splendour. The guests included the dancer, Serge Lifar, a descendent of a Doge, Prince Alexander of Yugoslavia, Princess Liechtenstein, Nancy Mitford, Madame

Schiaparelli among many other distinguished names. Flaming torches flickered on wrought-iron brackets on the walls reflected in the marble floor. The french windows were open onto the Grand Canal whence came the sound of water and singing gondoliers.

At dinner I remember that our son, David was seated between Gabrielle Liechtenstein, by this stage married to Mr. Kesselstat, but finding it more convenient to use the title gained from her first marriage, which was "The Princess of Liechtenstein". As soon as everyone was seated Gabrielle opened a conversation with Nancy Mitford across David, so to speak.

"They tell me, Miss Mitford, that you are writing a book on Frederick the Great?"

"I am, Princess."

"They also say, Miss Mitford, that you declare that he, the Emperor, spoke no German."

"That is so, Princess."

"That is not so, Princess. I do wonder whose sources you are using?"

After dinner our host led me to a small annexe. There was Nancy Mitford again, rather to his surprise, in the company of one other person who turned out to be my son Nevil! He was quite obviously having a hard time, and seized the first opportunity to shoot out of the shadowed room. He told me later that all his attempts to strike up a conversation had come to nothing, and they had been sitting in bored silence when we arrived. Presumably the great Miss Mitford had stalked into the second room and had remained sufficiently chagrined from the last encounter to refuse any further attempts at conversation.

That night John and I slept in a huge four-poster bed with gold brocades and in the next room David slept in a huge green bed over which hung a giant crucifix like a sword of Damocles. Nevil slept in a similarly imposing bedchamber.

Sadly, we were too briefly in Venice at that point to be able to take advantage of our hostess's considerable knowledge of Venetian painters – in particular of Carpaccio, on whom she is an expert. I can think of nothing more tempting that to revisit Venice and I have made several attempts to do so, but strangely, all have been abortive.

Inevitably, memory 'snatches' are inadequate, except for one quixotic one: after dining out with Italian friends of Jean and Belle de Nova, we wound our way home by footpaths and tiny canals, crossing the Piazza de San Marco, where a band was in full swing. Just at that moment, a tiny figure in black detached itself from a group of friends and began to dance, dance, in loveliness and total elegance. It was Serge Lifar the internationally famous French ballet dancer. Heavens, how he danced – and Venice slept.

Whatever the excitements of European adventures, it was always a delight to return to our beloved Geneva. There was of course a long history of English attachment to Switzerland. Through the centuries our countrymen had arrived there, intent on pursuing such diverse interests as painting and botany visits, if they were lucky. There was the famous visit of Maria Edgeworth to Marie-Auguste Pictet of the Bibliotèque Britannique. The of course there was de Candolle the botanist, closely linked with the English Systematists – and lastly but not least, the English mountaineers.

Picture of me at a party in Geneva, c.1969

So much for the English who unquestionably had a "special relationship". But what about the Portuguese, the Swedes and other EFTA members? Suffice it to say than the Genevois welcomed us all delightfully. We were shown aspects of the country not usually shared with foreigners.

Geneva was of course the international capital of Switzerland but Berne was the political centre. Paul Jollis was the equivalent of the President of the Board of Trade. He and Emma, his Greek wife, were keen art collectors, and their flat in Berne above the river was a treasure trove of contemporary art.

I will long remember a party given for Bridget Riley (the avant-garde artist), who was exhibiting at the Kloisters. After dinner it was suggested that we descend a spiral staircase to the flat of Berne's foremost art dealer, who wished to show us his treasures. As we emerged into a small room at the foot of the staircase, we faced a huge sculpture – in chocolate – of a Swiss cow. Bridget Riley did not hesitate; she instantly took a bite out of its flank. The scene can be imagined.

Not surprisingly I suppose Switzerland (and particularly the Suisse Romande or French speaking cantons) had, since the Second World War, become something of a popular refuge for the Royal families of Europe.

Although we had little or no connection where EFTA was concerned, due to our friends Jean and Belle de Noue, we were inevitably in touch with them from time to time, when Jean, as local Chef de Protocol for the UN would occasionally fit us into dinner parties to meet them. Jean was an inveterate snob and before such parties took place we were told how to behave! On one occasion, when we had just met the Queen of Italy

John supported by his two sons
at a friend's house in 1969

somewhere, he decided this was the moment to cash in on the situation, and 'ordered' us to call on her the next day at her small chateau outside Geneva. It was particularly difficult to fit this in and John had to lend me his chauffeur for the occasion. When we eventually arrived at Maylin, the chauffeur and I were somewhat startled as we drove into the royal precinct to find a substantial amount of removal lorries gathered near various entrances. Yes, it was a difficult situation – particularly as I could see John's youthful chauffeur doubled up with laughter at the totally unsuccessful efforts to find a way in to the little chateau.

Through glass panelling I could see shadowy figures and yes, surely it was the ex-queen herself flitting hither and thither, positively enjoying my discomfort. There was nothing for it but to reach for a wrought iron bell and pull with all my strength. I did so, and a tiny woman appeared out of nowhere and froze my blood. "Et qu'est ce que vous faites ici, madame?" This was too much, and I lost my head. " Je suis venue voir Madame la Reine," I heard a shivering whisper of a voice which could surely not be mine. But it was. In spite of a final visit (arranged of course by Jean de Noue) that close friendship which he obviously had in mind never progressed beyond a brief courtesy call. Alas, I am not made of the right stuff.

Before we left Geneva, EFTA laid on a magnificent Ball to say goodbye both to ourselves and to Eric and Lia von Sydow (at this point the Swedish Ambassador to EFTA and his wife). Our son David was also with us, having had a skiing accident some weeks before. As always on these occasions, there was a bitter-sweet element and I was reminded of something André de Blonay had said at a farewell lunch they gave for us some weeks earlier. André, who was Head of the Inter-Parliamentary Union and a fine musician, interrupted something I was saying about our hopeful plans to come back frequently to Geneva:

"Ah, Mavis! You may think you may be able to slip in and out of this city, on the basis of firm friendships as they exist today. But, ma chère, this is an illusion. From the moment you leave, our paths will inevitably diverge. Goodwill will remain, yes, but it will no longer remain possible to enjoy the day-to-day events you have shared with us. Inevitably, this is the end of a chapter".

Although I disagreed with him, André of course was right – but only up to a point. As I write this, nearly thirty years later, I still feel the special relationship we forged through EFTA and am still closely linked in warm friendship with Genevois friends. In fact, quite apart from EFTA, many other circumstances have contributed to this, the first being the "International Social Service" (ISS) with whom I have been closely associated, both in the UK and Geneva, for so many years; and the second? Well, I needed to pay regular visits with regard to the book I wrote after leaving, "Southwards to Geneva (200 Years of English Travellers)". And then, of course, together with Swedes, Americans, French and others, our Genevan "family" have visited us at our house, the Old Mill in Hampshire. Yes, the contact was and is maintained, and very precious it is. Alas, the same cannot be said about the EFTA organisation.

APRIL: GENEVA

In pollarded plane trees the blackbird tells
Of high mountainwisdom and cattle bells;
Of forsy this gold on medieval wall;
Of stinging bise and lake-flung squall;
Of shutters swung wide with orchestral zest;
Of an Alpine love which is always best;
Oh, always best.

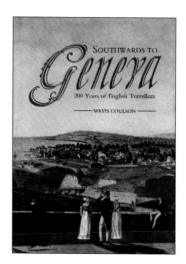

The cover of my book Southward to Geneva which was published in England in the early 1980s

94

CHAPTER NINE – *Retirement*

As soon as we had begun to readjust to life in Selborne, David, now nearly nineteen years old, announced that he was off to Africa, travelling with his camera. We had been rather looking forward to being with at least one of our sons in England. (Nevil was in New York with Schrobanco.) However, as we waited at Gatwick for his flight to be called – helped by a large gin-and-tonic – David told us he was leaving in order to make proper use of

The Old Mill, Selborne

his mental powers. This, of course, he has most certainly done.

Meanwhile, John was pushed by an old friend into becoming President of the Hampshire Red Cross, in succession to Lady Dorothy Malmesbury, who had just died. We had been connected, through friendships, with the hierarchy of the Swiss International Red Cross and had developed a huge admiration for the Swiss contribution. Although we had hardly begun to settle in at the Old Mill, John reluctantly agreed. Roger Sherfield, with whom we lunched a few days later, warned him on no account to be lured into "topping up some Old Cats' Home" – advice which, alas, came too late. Though in the event, of course, John was proud to be involved in this way and was lucky enough to have Betty Balfour, who had worked for years with the legendary Lady Dorothy, as his Director.

Here we were then – plunged, quite apart from the Red Cross, into a variety of local activities – connected at that moment largely with fund-raising for Selborne's church, running the annual fête and so on. Not before we had given ourselves a retirement present in the form of a month's holiday in Kenya.

John's old school had been Rugby – and Nevil had followed in his footsteps putting his name down for his old house and so on. When the time came, one September in the late 1950s, we were in Sweden, and John flew over to pick up Nevil from his prep school and take him there. On arrival he found that he was sharing a study with Peter Nightingale whose father had been at Rugby somewhat earlier than John and also at Whitelaw House. This was soon after the Mau Mau period, and Peter's parents were prominent members of the Settler Community in Kenya. The 'Winds of Change' were now blowing and it was decided that Billie Nightingale, his mother, should fly over to England to present the settlers' case to Ian McLeod, the Colonial Secretary, at the Lancaster House talks, and then proceed to Rugby to install their eldest son in his new venue. Billie told us of a conversation at Lancaster House which she had had with Jim Callaghan, the Prime Minister who succeeded Harold Wilson. Apparently Callaghan had said to Billie that by not cooperating, the settlers were merely knocking nails into their own coffins, to which Billie had replied, "Well, I hope you are coming to the funeral."

For three years, the two boys shared a ridiculously small study – and this was the beginning of a strong Nightingale/Coulson friendship. There were three younger children in Peter's family, and each year one would arrive in England for more advanced schooling. By arrangement, we would meet them at the airport, have them for the night, and generally keep an eye on them.

When the boys left Rugby, Nevil went with Peter to Kenya, just after Independence in 1963 – principally in order to climb Mount Kilimanjaro. Nevil was not particularly demonstrative by nature but on his return, he could not stop talking about Kenya because it had made such a big impression on him. Later his brother David also felt the draw of the country and within a few years, began making his own plans to reach the "promised land" including, of course, climbing Kilimanjaro too. He did so with Peter's younger brother, Richard, and they were later to travel to many wonderful places such as Lake Rudolf (now Lake Turkana, on the Ethiopian border) and Mozambique. When he first arrived the Nightingale parents put David up and for three months, at Billie's invitation, he was based on their turkey farm at Naivasha. By this time, David had completely fallen in love with Africa. It was during this time that John and I went to Kenya for the first time.

This was again a time of unrest in certain areas of Kenya. John, David and I went for the weekend to coffee and pyrethrum-growing friends of the Nightingales at Subukia, east of Nakuru, and found that their immediate neighbour was limping badly from an incident which had occurred some days before. Dick had been inspecting his coffee crop when he came across an outsize tractor (Kikuyu-driven) apparently performing a similar inspection on Dick's land. He shouted at the African in Swahili, asking what the hell he was up to. Whereupon the man drove the tractor straight at him, damaging his leg considerably.

This was only one of several worrying incidents, and as a result Tony Duff, our much-appreciated High Commissioner at the time, flew down to spend the night with our hosts, David and Kathleen Fielden, while we were with them, in order to bring comfort to local British farmers. Nearly everyone who came to meet him had, in order to show solidarity with the country of their adoption, taken out Kenyan citizenship at the end of

I'll never forget our first view of the
snow-capped crater of Kilimanjaro

Our son David, seen here in Northern Kenya
with Rendille warriors

On the Fieldens' farm at Subukia,
Kenya, in 1972

View from a friend's farm in Kenya, looking
out over the Great Rift Valley

the Mau Mau period. To their immense disappointment and frustration, Tony had to tell them that they could no longer call upon the British High Commission to protect them. As a result, several older farmers felt forced to leave.

Later that year, our David volunteered to drive Marian Taylor, a septuagenarian neighbour of both the Fieldens and the Nightingales, to Rhodesia. Marian had also had trouble on her farm and had opted to go south to join a nephew in the Rhodesian eastern highlands. The journey involved loading a VW Combi minibus with all Marian's worldly goods and six dogs (Dobermans and retrievers) and driving her two thousand miles to south Salisbury, then capital of Rhodesia, later Zimbabwe. Their ensuing adventures were colourful to say the least, and eventually David deposited his charge in Salisbury, where she was met by her nephew. He then proceeded to make his way to Johannesburg where he already had a few friends. This was the start of his new life in Africa.

We were very conscious when we were at Subukia with the Fieldens that their workforce was close to their house. There was something faintly disturbing in the air, and we were quite glad to return to the Nightingale Farm, where contact between their family and the workers still appeared reasonably friendly. The wives of white farmers all ran their own dispensaries, and one morning while we were there the Nightingale foreman arrived with his wife, who was behaving strangely. For no apparent reason, her eyes kept rolling backwards, and Billie could not make proper communication with her. In the end, her husband commented quietly that she had clearly been bewitched by an enemy who was determined to do her harm. It was agreed that another friendly witch-doctor should be consulted for a powerful antidote, and this was done. The foreman's wife recovered quite rapidly. (Alas, I cannot remember the mixture of herbs and roots involved).

Before we left Kenya, Billie and Ted took us on a home-made safari. Ted had been Governor of Equatorial Province of the Sudan and had spent much of his time in the bush. Both were as experienced as they were fearless. We spent our first night in a game-park lodge and heard in the distance a couple of lovesick lions roaring at each other. Very early next morning, Billie took us in search of them. We soon found them, furious at our interruption since they were intent on copulation. This took place four times, Billie pursuing them relentlessly. Finally, enough was enough, and the male turned on us. "Shut all the windows!" Billie shouted, as he charged. We did, with alacrity.

This was in 1972, and Kenya – beautiful though it was – showed the usual signs of poverty wherever one went. There were pathetic endeavours to sell home-grown fruit and vegetables – produce of faintly-glimpsed shambas (tiny plots) near "tourist" routes. Since then, with a son who has established his family in Kenya, we have paid many visits to a country which has an irresistible lure. Brilliantly beautiful as is South Africa, when I'm there I miss the sheer magnetism of Kenya – and the gentle kindness of so many Kenyans. I explain matters to myself – stupidly, no doubt – by acknowledging the part Kenya's geographic position must play. You are at the heart of the Equator here, and deeply involved in currents which have hardly changed since ancient times. All life is somehow affected by this Equatorial, almost umbilical cord.

During the ensuing years there were signs – slow but sure – of growing prosperity, as Kenya's international reputation improved and foreign companies began increasingly to invest in her. Politically, however, there was much uncertainty – and a few years ago, when I happened to be in Nairobi, the American Embassy was blown up. David's driver, Rom, was taking me to lunch with a friend who worked at the civil airport. Suddenly, all cars coming from the centre of Nairobi began flashing their lights. Rom instantly pulled off to the right of the road with "In Kenya, when this happens, it is a warning of some disaster!" On reaching the airport, I sought out Nicola, the AMREF representative there – only to find that within half an hour all offices had become small wards, and Kenyan ladies of all ages were on makeshift beds, giving blood. The behaviour of everyone was beyond praise. No panic; just a desire to help in all possible ways.

We were due to dine with a friend of Davids, the owner of a well-known Nairobi restaurant beside the American Embassy. He himself was flying back from South Africa and heard the news in mid-air. Although the Tamarind restaurant where we were due to dine had been partly destroyed he insisted on keeping the appointment with us at another restaurant he owned. In spite of the fact that both

John and I meeting a giraffe at the Giraffe Manor, Nairobi, Kenya

places seemed to have interchangeable staff and those waiting on us were obviously in a state of shock, the atmosphere was quietly controlled –reminding one strongly of the vaunted British phlegm.

* * *

And now the Hampshire wheel began to turn: the village school where I soon became a Governor was passing through a period of high dissatisfaction where the standard of Headship was concerned. Discipline appeared to have broken down with small boys out-of-hand and master-minded by a sinister adult who was encouraging them to become young burglars. Many Selbornian homes were broken into, and parents were vociferous in their call for a public meeting to air the whole situation. (The unfortunate headmistress was ill-equipped to deal with it, and there was no parental framework, as the school had never had a Parent/Teacher Organisation.) In the event, much good

John and I in Selborne in the 1970s with the mill behind

came out of this public meeting, as a PTA was rapidly formed, and not long afterwards the gentle head teacher left, in order to look after her ailing parents. A new head teacher was appointed by the Governors to take her place – and from then on, the school never looked back. Through the years (and my own governorship spanned all of twenty two years!), Selborne School flourished under a succession of first-class 'heads' – all of them much appreciated in their different ways.

The 'young burglars' in their time also turned their attention to our Norman church where they wreaked havoc by smothering the choir-stalls with graffiti, leaving a rather sinister pool on one of the altars, and so on. The Parish Council Committee became alarmed for the safety of our "priceless" 12 ft by 6 ft Flemish painting by Mabuse. This painting was hung over the altar, depicting as it did scenes of Mary and Jesus at Bethlehem, backed up by shepherds and Wise Men, with, as was customary, two donors at the side. Despite the fact that we were within a week of Easter, it was decided that the quite unprotected painting was most likely to be the next target of the young 'terrorists' who, with one squirt of graffiti mixture, could cause unthinkable damage. With one accord, we decided to remove the painting and after several abortive attempts to find a safe temporary home for it, we gratefully accepted an offer from the Anglican monks at Beech to hide it in the top gallery of their church. And there it remained, accompanied by cohorts of bats until a picture restorer working for the Council of Places of Worship came and executed a fine job on it.

Just before the Easter weekend, we pointed out to John Curtis, the Vicar, that for Good Friday and Easter Day there would be no 'Cross' in the background. A branch had recently broken off our Village Yew Tree in a storm. John Curtis strolled out to have a look at it, returning with two pieces of suitable lengths which he then nailed together. He placed the cross on the altar, where it remained until the return of the Mabuse painting. Meanwhile, so many people had remarked on what they found to be a very moving Cross that we decided to hang it just beyond the Chancel arch. I remember rifling my John's fishing tackle in order to make sure that the finest gut would obscure our suspension efforts.

In Selborne, meanwhile, village life chugged away peacefully, interspersed where we were concerned with occasional Foreign Embassy parties, visits to Covent Garden, Glyndebourne and innumerable plays and concerts. These activities were much helped by the existence of a tiny flat we had acquired in Westminster. This was only a hundred yards away from Parliament – and indeed, we were surrounded by MPs during the week. I used to hang my kitchen towels on the Division Bell in our minute kitchen. Sadly, it never rang for us! At this point, David returned from South Africa to take a crash course in Business Management, and here, of course, the little flat in Tufton Court came into its own.

Hampshire summers were peppered with fund-raising activities and, as John's wife, I had, ex officio, to be chairman of the annual Red Cross County Ball – a job I detested. At the end of the '80s, the Parish Council Committee felt that there should be

John in Selborne, not
long after he retired

Having tea in the garden with
the poet Tony Rye, c.1969

In the garden
with Bill Charlton

With my twin granddaughters, Daisy
and Alice, at Selborne in the mid 90s

Nevil's sons, Tim and Chris,
all smiles, in the late 80s

Presentation when I retired from the Board of Selborne School in the early 90's.

a historical event to mark the eight hundredth birthday of Selborne church and village. Accordingly, I wrote a play/pageant to that effect – with Natalie Mees as my archivist and Alistair Langlands as Producer. The then Bishop of Winchester, John Taylor, (he and his wife Peggy were great friends of ours) came for the event, and to everyone's delight, John Taylor took part in five performances. How fortunate we were to have the friendship of a bishop who seemed to combine so many gifts – strong spirituality, a first-class poet and playwright, writer, and remarkable historian!

'Selborne Story' was divided into fifteen episodes, and different village groups handled each section, with Newton Valence joining us for a particularly successful one. The play's action moved through the building of the transitional Norman church and onwards through history. The Youth Club, who were playing the part of pilgrims on their way to Canterbury, made a spectacular entry on ponies, trotting happily up the nave. Southern Television were eager to record this, and poured full lighting on the group. This was too much for the youngest and fattest pony bringing up the rear and he proceeded to discharge all he had into the nave. (Selborne nave is similar to so many old churches in that it is protected throughout its length by an iron grid.) Our vicar of the time, John Curtis, was a keen gardener, and appeared out of the blue with wheelbarrow and shovel

–claiming gardener's rights! The cast generally were superb, though the fact that we had two bishops (one an actor, one genuine) confused a rather small boy who ran into him at the grid, as he advanced from the South Door to give his re-dedication.of the Church. Gazing up at him with huge eyes, he touched John shyly: "Are you real?" he said.

Gilbert White (famous for his "The Natural History of Selborne") and his village have attracted, in addition to ecologists and Nature lovers, a whole collection of creative artists through the years. Not to be compared, of course, with Barbara Hepworth and St. Ives – but talented potters, wood engravers and that remarkable poet and writer, Tony Rye. The Rye family as a whole are a gifted lot. It must be said that Tony was as much a poet in person as he was on paper. While we were in Sweden, the Swedes brought out a translation of Gilbert White's "The Natural History of Selborne." We knew, of course, that this was in the offing – but it was a considerable surprise to open the paper one Sunday morning and find a double spread with an unmistakable drawing of Tony Rye sitting on a stool in our local bar, holding forth as he was wont to do. On the other side of this central double page was an extended article on the subject of Tony by the Swedish artist, Gunnar Brusewitz. It then appeared that Gunnar had been despatched to Hampshire on, I think, a two-month visit, to capture the spirit of Selborne – as it turned out, through the eyes of our local poet. We found ourselves rocking with laughter over a particular walk he had taken with Tony, their path, according to him, riddled with the ghosts of monks who once inhabited the Selborne priory.

Compared with friends in London, Selborne seemed a nest of intriguing characters – beginning with our remarkable butcher, "Mr Gallop". Mr Gallop spent much of the War in a bomb disposal unit, until the day when he saw that the bomb he was about to disarm was on the brink of exploding and disarming him. Instinctively he put his hands up to shield his face, with the result that he lost the fingers of both hands. He continued to practise his trade of butcher and became the love/fear of all children, his butcher's knives strapped to the hand-stumps he was left with. As may be imagined he became almost more widely known than Gilbert White.

From the age of 16 we knew young John Sole, his butcher-boy assistant. He used to cycle down our break-neck drive, bringing fish and meat when ordered. He was a red-headed lad, with whom we had one or two adventures.

In due course his courageous boss saw fit to retire; and who should take over the shop, but young (then rather less young, perhaps) John Sole. That was the time of the royal wedding and one morning, when I was buying cutlets or other delicacies, I saw John fairly bursting to communicate something. This went as follows: "M'lady," (that's what it was in those days) "she (his wife) is just off to Buckingham Palace with our wedding present – 3lbs of Royal Sausages!"

I did my best not to be impressed and enquired at what entrance she would be arriving. "Oh, the Queen's private secretary will be meeting her at the Royal Stables." "Really", I had to say, "how exciting!" It was. (Incidentally, Sue, John's delightful wife, reported that the private secretary was a "smashing gentleman"). We soon were all aware that something of importance was taking place. A lot of superannuated ladies had been recruited for the making of John's sausages on a grand scale, and several impressive white vans were seen ploughing their way through the country lanes, bearing appropriate legends.

My John was now well into retirement and so we had fewer 'diplomatic' invitations. However, the Swiss Embassy kindly asked us to dinner four nights before the Royal Wedding. All the buzz was about the Royal Wedding. John had been held up, so very soon dinner was announced. To my surprise and some amusement I found myself sitting next to the Queen's private secretary. Inevitably, the details of the wedding were discussed in the context of the presents, and I gently suggested the worries which must be involved with regard to certain gifts made – for example, the arrival of Royal Sausages freshly made. At which point the private secretary burst out: "Who on earth told you?" Who indeed?

Sad to say, John Sole suffered from what should have been an amusing, well-intentioned incident as well as an entrepreneurial triumph. Unaccountably, the sausages seemed not to be to the public taste and he found that he had seriously overstretched himself financially with this initiative. I am thankful to say, however, that he was made of strong stuff and has by now become a remarkably successful and well-known butcher.

In the centre of the village stands the Wakes, now a museum, but once the home of Gilbert White. It enjoys a magnificent aspect across its ha-ha to the trees on the Hanger. If there is a summer event – the village fete and many other occasions – people gather on the lawn of the Wakes.

One event was a jazz evening with Basil Moss and his colleagues delighting an audience who on the first evening did not know quite what to expect. It was an immediate success. Since then more and more people have become addicted to "Basil's Beat", bringing parties, picnics and retractable umbrellas – midsummer in England being interestingly uncertain.

Recently, Basil had an inescapable function on our chosen date. There was no getting round it and I don't know who was more disappointed, Basil or us. However, luckily for us the Kaleidoscopic "Trad jazz band", composed of jazz-linked friends and colleagues, nobly stepped in and proved a worthy replacement. Applications for tickets continued to pour in, until, at over 600, we felt we would have to call a halt. Meanwhile, advance parties began arriving to set up their picnics. Through the years many of these had risen in grandeur – from a rug on the ground and sandwiches to trestle tables laden with ambitious-looking buffets (shades of Glyndebourne.). Authentic noises began emerging from the jazz tent. A saxophone let out a groan and "suddenly they were off."

By this time we were seated, helping ourselves to goodies, and I was endeavouring to explain to the charming young Hungarian ambassador how the English did things. The next moment the heavens discharged the biggest cloud-burst I had ever seen. A self-sacrificing couple shot off (home presumably?), returning with fistfuls of golfing umbrellas. The evening went on, food consumption being somewhat erratic as holding a golf umbrella with one hand and dissecting meat with the other is an acrobatic feat. What was more, as we sat, stood and clapped, a collective decision was taken on our table that dancing is the only way to dry up, so…let's go. and we did – with our umbrellas.

The Kaleidoscopic group were in fine form. After all, their solid tent kept them splendidly dry. And, where watching their dripping audience take to the floor (i.e. grass) was concerned, they had seats in the stalls. Yes, it was a tremendous evening, the joy and panache exceeding any Hungarian or Slavonic dance.

Such is the stuff which forms the English: the backcloth of a picturesque village, torrential rain in summer, an undaunted spirit in adversity and a shared spirit of adventure which somehow surpasses the excitement of the event itself. No wonder so many who wander round the world most of their lives are drawn home as if by a magnetic force to live out their days in such a special place – the English village!

The sitting room at Upstream where I moved after John's death in 1997

Steephill Castle on the Isle of Wight, home of the Hanborough family

Sybil Hanborough

One of our Steephill ancestors

Verner family group in
the Victorian era

Appendix 1 – *The Hambroughs*

In 1828, one hundred and seventy six years ago at the time of writing, my great great grandfather, John Hambrough, who was already owner of estates at Pipewell Hall, Marchwood Lodge and, most recently, Farringford Hall, Hampshire, bought an estate at Ventnor, Isle of Wight, from Lord Dysart's family as a present for his much-beloved wife Sophia Townsend, of Honington Hall, whom he had married in Warwickshire in 1820. The building of Steephill Castle, in simulation of a medieval, crenelated castle, began at once, and became a thriving family home. My grandmother Catherine Hambrough (Aunt Cassie) and her siblings grew up there, in what must have been an idyllic childhood. Catherine and one of her sisters were both to marry into the Verner family, of County Armagh in Ireland. This was a family of some distinction, owning a huge estate and having an ancestor, Sir William Verner, who was said to have been the person who announced the news of the Battle of Waterloo at the famous Brussels Ball. Apparently one Verner brother met one older Hambrough daughter, became engaged, and subsequently introduced his bride-to-be to his confirmed-bachelor brother who remarked, "Well, if I ever found another girl like that I would consider getting married too." Later, this brother met his sisters-in-law, unaware that the Hambroughs had plans to marry off one of the next daughters in line to this Verner brother. While he was in the servants' courtyard he saw the youngest daughter, Catherine, who was barely sixteen, peeping through the banisters at him. She dropped a handkerchief through the banisters and whispered, "Are you a bachelor?" The astonished Verner picked up the handkerchief and raised his eyes to look at his questioner and that was it! Catherine's husband eventually became a judge in Rawalpindi, but his wife was not typical of a Judge's spouse, being rather fey, and having far more interest in veterinary matters than feminine accomplishments and social status. As proof of this, when Catherine and her husband sailed out to India, they brought with them a set of metal trunks which contained her wedding trousseau, carefully packed for Catherine by her sisters. On their return from the East, years later, back came all these tin trunks, and they had never even been opened.

Poor John Hambrough, who originally built Steephill Castle, had, alas, went blind at the age of forty, and was never able to see the castle as a finished creation. The years went by and, in spite of occasional misfortunes, life, from what one can gather, was full of social events, embracing visits from Queen Victoria and her family, friendships with the Tennysons and so on. Of the children born to John Hambrough and his wife Sophia, there were, I think, four girls and three younger sons – the eldest of whom, Cedric, was

James Verner in the uniform of
the 19th Dragoons.

My great grandmother,
Charlotte Verner, nee May

a lad of seventeen in 1893, recently commissioned into the Army, and the apple of his
father's eye. No expense was spared to give him the experience necessary for a young man
of his age and background. A tutor, Alfred Monson, was engaged to escort him to
Scotland, where he was to be taught to shoot. There followed a hideous story, whereby
Monson and a 'third man', assumed by witnesses to be a betting agent, initially endeavoured
to drown Cedric, who could not swim. For this purpose, a hole had been drilled in the bottom
of their boat. Miraculously, however, Cedric managed to reach land before the boat sank
– only to be found next day in woodland, shot through the head, or so the story went.

Although the evidence pointed to an arranged murder by Monson and his
bookmaker friend, Monson alone stood in the dock, Edward Sweeney, alias Davis, alias
Scot, having vanished almost immediately. Due apparently to the incompetence of certain
proceedings during the trial, the case under Scottish law was designated 'not proven', which
permitted Monson to walk away a free man.,

Cedric's father, Dudley Albert, never recovered from the death of his much-loved
son. According to my mother, he lost interest in life, and this resulted in the breakdown
of family life at Steephill. Cedric's brothers were still in early childhood but the girls, who
had their own lady's maid, had to rely wherever possible on the kindness of aunts and

uncles to take them in. Looking through the family list of names (found on the Internet), I recognise several connected with the Hambrough/Verner family, known to me in my youth – though at that age, of course, I was quite uninterested in their background.

For example, Sybil Hambrough: she was adopted by my Verner grandparents at the age of thirteen. (She and Amy, my mother, were exactly the same age, and were inseparable.) She became my Godmother, and apparently, from an early age, showed what must have been a vocational desire to devote her life to caring for the under-privileged – largely in the East End of London.

Then there was Aunt Ethel – rescued by Aunt Charlotte Mary (first daughter of Albert John) to marry and leave home. I must have been about three years old when my mother Amy took me to stay with Aunt Mary in a Regency house in Bath. She had been widowed and lived in the Crescent, I think. (I seem to remember that there were handsome black railings everywhere.) At the time of the Hambrough disaster, Aunt Mary took in a rather disturbing younger sister. Even to a three-year-old, Aunt Ethel was disturbing. She floated round the house dressed in lilac muslin, and fairly choked the atmosphere with lavender! Above all – and this worried me terribly – she had a beloved dog (a large specimen of highland terrier with enormous ears.) Aunt Ethel would put this animal to bed each night in a real wooden bed with sheets and blankets! There was something almost outrageous about this and although she would lovingly hold me up at the window behind the dog's bed, to see the twinkling lights of Bath, I was never, no, never at ease with her. When I was older, I seem to remember our mother murmuring that poor Auntie Ethel had only been married for one night.

Then there was Millicent, who escaped by marrying the Vicar of Thursley. To me he was quite terrifying. They came and spent a night with us at the White House, bringing with them their small daughter Mary – four years older than me. There was something of the night about him, I found; and even now I can conjure up his intensely tall figure, permanently dressed in black. Our parents asked him to lead the prayers – a pre-breakfast ritual- where the staff filed in according to rank and (normally) our father, Edwin, read from the Bible. There was something false in the way Uncle 'A' officiated – long-fingered, hairy hands gesticulating dramatically.

Mary and I played happily together despite the four year difference in age. (The gap seemed huge to me.) In due course my mother and I were asked to spend a weekend at Uncle 'A's vicarage. Mary's father clearly liked small girls, and attempted to ingratiate himself with me by putting horrid hairy fingers down my liberty-bodice-encased back, in order to post me a half crown. Ugh!

I think it must have been three years or so later when, in order to make room for Millicent's successor, he threw out Millicent and Mary – following this up later by setting fire to the vicarage and claiming the resultant insurance compensation.

This act confirmed the feeling of disgust within the whole family, and united everyone in attempts to help the unfortunate Millicent. She, it must be said, showed extraordinary courage – helped again by various members of the family. Determined that Mary should receive an excellent education, she applied to Benenden School in Kent, offering her services as, I think, a house-matron, in order to have free lodging for them both. To the astonishment of the family she was accepted as a member of staff! Millicent was no academic and was therefore determined that Mary should leave school with the credits she herself lacked and which she so much wanted for her daughter. Mary duly left school with these credits and, two or three years later, married Derick Hoare, a partner in Hoare's Bank. (My mother had included her in a party she arranged before a local dance organised by aunts of Derick.) Derick became Lord Mayor of London in 1961, following in the footsteps of an earlier Hoare in the late eighteenth century. Mary herself ultimately founded The Lady Mary Hoare Thalidomide Trust. One of her two daughters is my god-daughter.

APPENDIX 2 – *The Legend of Santa Lucia*

This legend tells the story of a young girl named Maria who lived with a bellicose father in the heart of a forest in north-west Sweden. The father decides to go to the help of a distant neighbour who is being attacked by ruthless marauders. He takes with him all of his men and leaves his daughter in charge of his snow-bound house. Before leaving, he shows her the emergency wine and food which he has set aside for their return – of which he knows they will be in dire need. Time passes, and one night a little group of erstwhile farmers announce their presence with feeble knocking on the door. Maria finds an exhausted company of beaten-up and starving neighbours. She is desperate to find them food and drink but all there is in the house is the stock reserved for the return of her father and his men. She hurriedly goes to the cellar and extracts a little food and one large pitcher of wine. She soon realises that this is quite inadequate so she comes back for more. The wine is running out fast, and, to her horror, she hears noises indicating that her father and his company have actually returned. The next minute he is standing before her, red in the face with fury.

"Fetch me one bottle of wine which isn't empty!" he shouts. And with the butt of his rifle he sends her reeling backwards. Maria picks up the jug he had been holding and vanishes down into the cellar. She knows that her father will stop at nothing when roused thus, but as she weeps she becomes aware that the jug she carries has become much heavier. A sweet-voiced girl is telling her not to be afraid – that she, Santa Lucia, will protect and take care of her, and see that she is not bullied by her father. Sure enough, Maria is vaguely aware of a presence and the pitcher she holds always remains two thirds full of wine. Her father, seeing that everything in his household seems to have settled down normally, ceases to persecute her. But in that Swedish forest from then on it is recognised that Santa Lucia has made herself known as the champion of the persecuted and her story gradually becomes one of Sweden's most popular legends. There are various versions of the legends. This one is contributed by Selma Lagerlöf, the well-known children's author. Every year on December 13th, regarded as the darkest night of winter, there are commemorative small processions when, in every household or business, the blondest girl is chosen to represent Santa Lucia.

Margaret's Story

Margaret's Story – CHAPTER ONE

The girl watched the French coast recede into early morning mist. Heavily pregnant, she leaned clumsily against the ship's rail – oblivious of screaming gulls above and around her.

Muriel was not normally introspective. Now, though, as she gazed automatically into the ship's wake, she seemed to see events of the last 18 months ticker-taping through the parting waves.

Heaven knew she had never wanted to go to Ceylon. After her mother had died, she and her father had settled down to a comfortably bourgeois life together. Without ambition, and pathologically shy at the mere appearance of a young man, she had been perfectly content to fill her days with golf and the occasional visit to cousins in Norfolk. It was that ball at the Longrishes which had set the whole thing in motion. The Longrishes were old friends of her parents, and she had been at school with Annabel, their second daughter. Annabel had never been her type; and when Muriel's father told her he had accepted an invitation to her 21st birthday ball, Muriel had known the evening would be a disaster. Events had proved her only too right. Eighteenth century Bracken Hall was of course perfect for the occasion. What was more, Annabel's parents were excellent hosts – and Muriel secretly admired the brother Eustace. All the more horrible, then, that she had never collected a single dance-partner for her programme! The nightmare had been extended as she sat beside the ball-room floor – classic Victorian wallflower – watching in mortification Rosie and Violet, also at school with her, as they whirled by on the arms of their partners – faces vapidly happy. It had been particularly cruel, she felt, because she knew she was in rather good looks that night. Taking a quick glance in the looking-glass before leaving their house, she had seen a healthy – yes, almost handsome young face gazing back at her. Nothing to write home about but still… nothing to be ashamed of, either. With her chestnut hair, strong features and shy hazel eyes, she had, she felt, considerable assets. If only she could conquer her terror of young men.

Miserably she had sat beside the dance floor until her father, who on arrival had quickly vanished into the smoking-room, had emerged and found her there. Instantly he had whisked her off to supper and, seeing her stricken face, had devoted himself to her for the rest of the evening. She knew it was then that he had decided to take her to stay with Lettice in Ceylon. Poor Father! He meant well, of course – but was totally unable to understand that the mere thought of being dangled in front of all Robert's brother officers was anathema to her. The 'Fishing Fleet' That's what they called the P&O boats plying their way between England and Bombay and thence to Colombo. She shuddered in recollection, seeing the decks of HMS Reliance crammed with unmarried girls, chaperoned by their families and destined to be thrown as bait to any young man who would have them.

How disastrous it had all been! She could see them now – her sister Lettice, the children, Charlie and Louise and their ayah – waiting on the quayside at Colombo as the ship docked. Lettice, with their mother's finely-chiselled features, and natural elegance! ("Knows how to dress, that girl", her father had muttered). "Papa, Muriel! How delightful to see you! Did you have a good voyage? I'm afraid Edward could not be here… A polo match, you know. The colonel insisted…" The voice spoke quickly and nervously, as its owner piloted them towards the waiting carriage. Their luggage had already been taken in hand by Rani, the Ceylonese servant. He loaded it into a second smaller vehicle, and now, turning to them with a little bow, helped them take their places in the main carriage. What a journey that had been! It was Muriel's first experience of humid heat. The coach was insufferably hot, and the roads scored with deep ruts. While her father and Lettice exchanged news she tried shyly and unsuccessfully to engage Charlie and Louise in conversation. They replied only in monosyllables – sitting opposite like stiff little dolls, and eyeing her obliquely. It was a relief when the road began to climb steeply, for now the air became cooler and, from the carriage windows, there were glimpses of brilliantly green tea-gardens. They reached the bungalow late in the evening, and in spite of herself Muriel was instantly charmed by its long, low lines and terrace awash with bougainvillea. Lettice, elegant and aloof as she had always been, showed them their rooms. Edward appeared later, fresh from polo: Edward with his dark, aquiline good looks and darting eyes. He had been politely interested in their journey; she well remembered, though, being surprised at the perfunctory way in which he and Lettice addressed each other.

The next weeks flew by – with picnics, polo, visits to tea-gardens, and several days spent in Kandy. One afternoon, they were in the Temple and she accidentally found herself alone with Edward in a little shrine. Their guide moved on ahead with the rest of the group. Edward suddenly took her arm and squeezed it. She found herself tingling at the experience, and did not move away from him. "Muriel", he murmured: "I…my dear! I need to see you by yourself. To-night…after dinner…in the garden…under the giant jacaranda. I'll wait for you…" He was trembling, she remembered. At that moment Lettice's voice called – "Muriel, Edward.' Wherever are you? The temple is closing… We must all leave."

She could smell now the scent of the jacaranda flowers that night. How astonishing that her father's well-brought up unmarried daughter – his pet – should have been so hypnotised. She, hitherto so terrified by young men! All her concentration had been on getting through dinner that night, and managing to elude her family. For one moment, as she rose from her seat on the verandah, it looked as if her father would join her. But on hearing that she just wanted a short stroll ("the scents are marvellous, and the air so much cooler now"), he let her go. And Edward, who had left the table at the end of dinner on pretext of joining some brother officers in Kandy – Edward was waiting for her. It was very dark under the jacaranda tree. She saw nothing from beginning to end: only felt. First, his arms clasping her, as if he were on the edge of drowning; then the rain of kisses; then some Victorian padlock inside her bursting open … her own hot kisses. And then, then total abandonment – with Edward showing her everything and she herself caught up in the frenzy of it all.

How she made her way to her room in the by-now-nearly-silent bungalow - answering her father's "Where the deuce are you, Muriel?" as he searched for her in the garden with a "I must have dozed off under the trees, father, and am just going to bed", she would never know. Waking the next morning, she had been consumed with guilt – dreading to meet the family and sure that her behaviour must be branded all over her. To her astonishment, life went on as usual. Her father, glancing at her that evening, remarked that the climate seemed to suit her…that she was positively in good looks (unheard of praise from him!). He went on to caution her about lingering under the tropical trees at night… and that was all. Edward had been out all day, and when she did meet him at dinner, it was clear that he was avoiding her. At the end of the week, they all returned to Nuwera Eliya, and he and his platoon were sent to Trincamalee, on the East coast. Subsequently, during the weeks before she and her father sailed for England, they hardly met.

The voyage home had been a nightmare of horror. Her father was determined that she should meet and dance with as many young officers as possible. He had now become obsessional on the subject and was mortified that Ceylon had failed to produce a single aspirant for Muriel's hand. The ship was loaded with officers returning home on leave. Each night, when the dancing began, Grant Wollen would sit hopefully with his daughter near the dance-floor. Occasionally, some young man would present himself and whirl her off for a dance. But Muriel's shyness – made worse by an uneasy feeling of being somehow unclean, had kept them all at arms' length. All, that is, except a sad-looking ensign of spotty complexion. It appeared he had recently lost his fiancée in a typhus epidemic and was inconsolable. Muriel and he presented no threat to each other, and it was a comfort to be able to dance the occasional waltz with him, and later take a stroll round the deck.

As the ship left the Mediterranean, she began to be aware that her waist was thickening…that things were not as they should be. She was seized with sudden terror.

Is this what happened to girls when they…when they…did what Edward and she had done? Surely it was not possible that such things could happen in such a short time? Muriel was not only a child of her time where sex was concerned but also motherless. Her innocence was therefore total, and, passionate as that brief moment with Edward had been, (leaving her with feelings of euphoria mixed with guilt) she had never dreamed of possible consequences. What had Father said at breakfast that morning? "Muriel, my dear, you seem to be putting on a certain amount of weight. Unhealthy life, this, on board ship! The sooner we're home and you're back on the golf course the better. And take my advice – avoid the cakes and scones at teatime!"

Margaret's Story – CHAPTER TWO

Their return home to Dorking had been of course a mixed blessing. The house, large and Victorian, was without great architectural pretensions. But it was the home she had always known and childishly she had cherished the hope that, once in the old routine, she would be able somehow to say goodbye to the nightmare. Life resumed its normal pattern. There were the usual social activities; occasional visits to relatives; the theatre in London. And golf! How she adored her golf! Muriel was a healthy, unimaginative girl, with a love of the outdoors and small interest in books. Brought up in late Victorian society, she could not imagine her father's reactions to her situation. What was she to do when the inevitable happened? Above all, what would HE do – this doting father of hers – when concealment was no longer possible?

The blow fell when they were returning from the golf-course one day. Uncharacteristically she had played disgracefully and her father told her so without mincing words. As they came through the drive-gates, he handed her a club ordering her to make a few practice swings on the lawn. He watched her critically and, quite suddenly, hurried her up the steps of the house and into the morning-room. Embarrassed and highly emotional, he began raining questions. Her terrified answers only confirmed his worst suspicions. The fact that his own son-in-law should be father to the child within her was too much for him. He broke down, and left the room. Muriel had supper alone that night, and, in a state of misery (for she was devoted to her father) went to bed early.

In the morning her father barely greeted her at breakfast – leaving the room shortly after her appearance. Later, she heard him slam the front door. Paula, the parlour maid, looked at her quizzically, saying he had gone to London and did not know when he would be back. In fact, he returned twenty four hours later. Bradshaw the coachman drove to meet him at the station. She watched him alight and walk up the front steps – wearing the air of a man who has decided much.

"You will prepare your luggage at once" he told her that night, averting his face. "And buy…er…anything you are likely to need for the next two and a half months. Mrs. Bradshaw (the housekeeper who had been with them since the death of Muriel's mother) is…ah…aware of your situation. She will help you. We will leave for Benoit, near Bourges, in France. There we shall stay till…till…" He did not finish his sentence. "After that, I have made arrangements…"

Well, Benoit had turned out to be a not-unattractive small town, with its late-medieval Place and narrow, shuttered streets. The Hotel de France was next door to the

Mairie and quiet and inoffensive. Mr Wollen had reserved the second floor. He and Muriel had rooms leading off a small central salon.

For some days Muriel felt like a sleep-walker. The nightmare was growing, together with her child. Although it was a relief that her father knew, and had taken charge of the situation, she had no clear idea of the future. Her mother had died when she was eight. She and Lettice had been brought up by an old nurse, with their father severely in the background. At best, Victorian girls were ill-prepared for life by their mothers; and in this case the sisters were totally ignorant of sex. Before leaving England for Benoit, her father had summoned the family doctor. Dr D had examined her thoroughly, said the child in her womb seemed healthy and had given the likely date of birth as the end of June – in four months time. "That is, if you behave prudently," he added. He had looked long at her, sighed heavily, and gone away shaking his head. He and her father had had a prolonged conversation in the hall. She had heard their murmured voices.

After a week or so, a routine was established in their life at Benoit. The morning was spent idly. Grant wrote letters, informing all his friends and business acquaintances that he and Muriel had decided to take a holiday, and would be spending the next few months in France. While he was at his desk, Muriel would do her needlepoint. As she did so, she would speculate on the future. Not daring to ask her father what plans he had made for her, she would sometimes drop her work and stare unseeingly at the heavy mahogany table ahead of her. What would happen when the child was born? She believed childbirth was terrible. And even, as seemed likely in view of her excellent health, she survived the pain and indignity, what then? It was inconceivable that she should keep the baby. The idea never even entered her head. No, undoubtedly it must be adopted – and as soon as possible. Once, long ago, Nurse had spoken of a young couple who had longed to have a child, but for some reason were unsuccessful. They had been made happy, she remembered, by the arrival of a baby from the orphanage. Well, then! Somebody would be only too glad to have hers – and the problem would be solved. Unless…unless…the baby might of course be born…dead. Would that not be the best solution?

She became preoccupied with the thought – until one day the little maid who waited on them failed to appear with their breakfast. When Muriel enquired about her, she learned from the housekeeper, who spoke a little English, that Clairette had been very foolish… had tried to do away with a baby 'conceived in the straw, you understand, Madame…', was now very ill, and unlikely to recover, the doctor said. Mme Barbet, the housekeeper, looked closely at Muriel as she spoke – and shortly afterwards, asked with elaborate carelessness whether they would soon have the pleasure of meeting Madame's husband.

After that, Muriel thought no more of abortion: only of the blessed day when the child would be born naturally, and she could be rid of it.

Time went on. She and Grant would take a walk each afternoon, or make occasional visits to neighbouring towns and medieval churches. Her father, whose joy in life she was, could not long keep up his outraged silence. One afternoon, as they were leaving the cathedral in Bourges, he took her arm and began to outline to her his plans for the future. Through a friend, he had discovered an excellent gynaecologist in Vichy. He was already in touch with him, and next week they would go to see him. He had, it appeared, a nursing home, and everything would be arranged comfortably. After that, he had plans for the child. Muriel had no idea what these were…and had not the courage to pursue the matter further.

They were returning from a stroll the following afternoon, and had stopped momentarily outside a maroquinerie opposite their hotel. Mr Wollen was considering the purchase of a small brown valise. They were discussing its merits… Suddenly an English voice broke in on their conversation. "Wollen, old man! You of all people! and Muriel, too! What an extraordinary thing to find you here! I'm on my way to Vichy… Am stopping here overnight to see Gaston Pivet… Remember him? He was at Trinity with us. But my dear old fellow, you must meet him. Has some kind of château near here. But of course you must dine with us tonight! He is coming to my hotel – l'Hotel de France."

That chance meeting had of course destroyed all her father's carefully laid plans. He was frozen with horror at Jocelyn Booth's sudden appearance …attempting to distract his attention from Muriel's now swollen form as they shook hands…making excuses for her at dinner that night, on the grounds of a sudden chill. Next day, white and looking twenty years older, he had met her at breakfast. "Muriel, we are leaving at once – at once, do you hear? I cannot run any further risk… We will return to England, travelling by night as far as possible. I find there is a ferry leaving tomorrow night from Calais. Once over the Channel I will make new arrangements".

Staring into the ship's wake, Muriel was unaware of the early morning scene. The coast of France was faintly visible in the early morning mist. Close behind her, the Dover cliffs shone white in first sunlight. Gulls were flocking round the ship – filling the air with harsh cries. Grant's words, in the train to Calais the day before rang in her ears. "You can trust me, Muriel. Indeed, I am convinced that you know that (here he looked at her with ill-concealed tenderness) I shall soon have matters in hand, you'll see!" Poor Father! He had pressed her hand, before turning away to wipe his brow surreptitiously.

Grant Wollen sat at a large, mock-Empire desk, beside an open window. The sea was visible beyond the roof-tops ahead, though he had no eyes for it. Below, in a busy street, the town of Boulogne went about its business and cries rose from the market round the corner.

He was half way through a pile of postcards, addressed to his friends and family. "M. and I just off on what should be a splendid tour of Florence, the Italian Lakes, etc., etc. All a last-minute decision. Couldn't miss a unique opportunity to join cousins…" He continued to write, in similar vein. Finally, he sat long before an empty sheet of paper …began to write several times – and finally committed himself. When finished, the letter read as follows:

"My dear Frances,

(Forgive me, but I still cannot quite conceive of you as Sister Frances!) It is twelve years since your kind and sympathetic letter, written on the death of my dear wife, gave me news that you had been promoted to 'No. 1' at the Convent of the Holy Child near Hemel Hempstead: news which held little surprise to all who knew you and were aware of your exceptional abilities.

I write now to you, old friend, in what amounts to some desperation. To be brief, the unmentionable, the disastrous, has occurred. Muriel has become pregnant by her sister's husband. Yes, is it not too horrible?" (Here, Grant Wollen paused, and passed a handkerchief over his face). "These wretched circumstances arose because I arranged to take Muriel to spend some months with Lettice and her family, in Ceylon. Lettice's husband, Edward, is with his regiment – guarding Government House in Nuwera Eliya, in fact. They lead a lively life, Muriel is now nearly twenty one and I felt it time that she extended her acquaintance. In short, I hoped, I suppose, that in such surroundings she would meet some eligible young soldier. So much for my plans. In the event, she took no interest in any of the young subalterns who were constantly in and out of the house. Rather, after a certain time, she seemed to go out of her way to avoid the little attentions that many of them paid her. I was somewhat put out, I must confess, and even more so during the return voyage, when exactly the same thing occurred. After all, the conditions there were all that a young, unattached girl could desire. Plenty of young men, Indian Ocean under a full moon. Ah, my dear old friend. I am an old man now – and a lifetime away from youthful feelings of romance. But I confess to you that the atmosphere took me back forty years and more – to a Scottish ball – and a walk by a loch at dawn with someone very dear to me. Elysium seemed to lie before me then, Frances. But what am I saying? Forgive me, my dear! Memories are too strong, and I succumbed to them".

You will understand my frustration, therefore, when Muriel seemed uninterested in any of the young men who presented themselves for a dance – with the exception of some wretched and exceptionally plain young widower, in whose company she clearly felt safe. I put it all down, of course, to her unusual shyness where young men are concerned; and indeed was largely correct in my estimation. It was not until our return to England that the monstrous truth finally forced itself upon my attention.

As you may imagine, I took instant steps to prevent her dishonour. She and I removed to a small village in France, where we would have remained until the end of her term, had not our seclusion been broken by the arrival of a talkative and unreliable acquaintance. As it was, I could not risk inevitable discovery, and we immediately returned to Dorking. Muriel is now at Wareham in Sussex, where I have rented a small house until the deplorable matter is finished.

I am arranging to engage the services of the best accoucheur in Harley Street. A midwife will join us in due course, and I shall naturally make the necessary arrangements after the birth. But now, I throw myself on your mercy, my dear Frances, and am about to put our old, close friendship to the ultimate test. Would you, in all the special circumstances, consent to become godmother to the child, and, as godmother, would you take this child into your convent and bring her up as such?

I dread to receive a refusal from you. To whom, otherwise, can I turn? I beg you, dear friend, for the sake of what is past, help a shattered father overcome his daughter's dishonour?

Your affectionate old friend, etc…"

The convent hall, used partly as a living-room by the nuns, was large and sparsely furnished. A small group of sisters fluttered round the occupant of a wheelchair, while a little girl danced for their entertainment. Her light-brown ringlets swung wildly as she skipped, gestured and pirouetted. The nuns clapped warmly and the child finished with a deep curtsey to the chair-bound figure.

"Now, Margaret, Sister Bertha is waiting to take you to your dancing lesson. Run and get your coat, now.'" The older nun spoke briskly and as the small girl skipped out of the room, she turned with half-reproving smile to the nun about to follow her: "Sister, try to be a little stricter with her! Margaret can twist you round her little finger." Sister Bertha blushed and nodded: "I know, Mother, I know. But there is something so charming, so …vivid, that severity seems impossible." She smiled self-deprecatingly and left the room. The Mother Superior's eyes followed her. They wore a thoughtful expression. "Sister Joan," she remarked, when the other nuns had dispersed and the sister behind her chair had pushed her over to a little table in the corner of the room, "how greatly things have changed with us during the last few years – changed for the better, I mean! You came to St. Andrew's, I suppose, about fifteen years ago?" The sister nodded. "You well remember, then our quiet ways in those days. Nothing like you would find in a contemplative order, of course. No", with a little laugh, "our class-rooms are very far from quiet! Healthily noisy, I suppose you'd call them – with all that pent-up energy which the very young must dispose of. I was referring rather to the rhythm of our own lives in the convent. We had become, perhaps, a little set in our ways – pursuing innocently our daily round of prayer and praise of the dear Lord without, I am inclined to think, much human touch. And then, Margaret arrived! Thank you, Sister Joan, I am quite comfortable now. I need my book of Compline, though – and yes, my spectacles. I left them on my desk a little earlier. Oh, and perhaps you would find Sister Hilary for me, and tell her I want to see her after the Office. It's about the Sixth Form curriculum." Sister Joan hurried out, while Mother Frances continued with her train of thought.

Yes, it must be more than six years since Margaret had arrived amongst them. She would never forget the day that Grant Wollen's letter arrived. Mr Wollen, who had been partly responsible for her decision to become a nun. Even now the emotions of fifty odd years ago threatened to overcome her and she saw again the loch in the grey light of early morning. They were playing the Gay Gordons up at the house. She was walking on the shore with Grant Wollen – only half listening to the torrent of love-talk which poured from him. Only half-listening because her mind and whole being yearned to be with Harry. She had loved Harry from the moment they had met, at last year's Games. And tonight he had told her that he had proposed to Blanche, and it seemed that Blanche – her close friend – had accepted him. Dear Grant. He was so devoted, and she was very fond of him. But…indeed he was not Harry, and all too clearly she saw there never could be another Harry. Firmly she had disengaged herself from Grant Wollen, who was pulling her to him. Before he could stop her, she had run towards the house – her mind made up. Some hours later, instead of joining the others for a late breakfast, she had set off on foot for the station, three miles away. Luck had been on her side for she had met no one. The lunch-time train for the Midlands and London was punctual and by late afternoon she was nearing King's Cross. It was dark by the time she reached St Andrew's Convent in Berkshire. Her aunt, who had brought her up, had a friend there – an old nun. What an apparition she must have presented that night: hammering on the convent door in her blue crinoline. They had been wonderful to her, she remembered – bringing supper to her in the tiny room she had been allocated and asking no questions. Left to herself for the night she had begun in exhaustion to remove her clothes – realising only then the utter impossibility of unfastening her crinoline – a task performed always by Beth, her maid. Despite the discomfort, she had slept fitfully – worn out by emotion.

Mr Wollen's letter had shaken Sister Frances. That poor child Muriel! The situation was indeed a nightmare for father and daughter. She could see it all: Mr Wollen who, unless he had changed in all those years, attached exceptional importance to social status; the girl Muriel. A little gauche, perhaps, and certainly shy… She must be quite crushed. It was probable that she entertained no feelings of motherhood, and relied totally on her father to make all arrangements. But, finding suitable adoptive parents in such a situation was one thing. Sending a very young baby to be brought up in a convent, quite another! She remembered how she had prayed about it – how they had all prayed. For of course she had presented the problem to the sisters – knowing that any step of such importance must be a community decision. A baby in the convent! Sister Teresa had greeted the possibility with uninhibited delight, Sister Ella with caution. What, she pondered anxiously, would become of their peaceful rhythm of existence? Sister Bertha, St Andrew's moody, unpredictable history teacher, had of course forecast disaster should such a step be taken. It was at this point that Sister Frances had painted a picture for them of an unwilling mother-to-be and the unwanted child she was carrying. What was to happen to this rejected scrap of humanity, she had asked? Rather than seeking to preserve the tranquillity of convent lives, should they not perhaps regard it as their duty to respond to this most unusual challenge? Her words had produced their effect. After further prayer the Lord had guided them and the decision had been made – not, however, without extreme reluctance on the part of Sister Bertha.

The wrinkled face of Sister Frances lit up with an amused smile. God did indeed move in mysterious ways. Sister Bertha was unquestionably one of His Wonders. Who could have guessed that a month-old baby's arrival at the convent would in time have transformed this short-tempered, difficult sister into the loving, doting (that was the word for it) creature who waited on Margaret at every moment she was free from the classroom? When Mr Wollen had arrived with the child, Bertha had absented herself from the little group of nuns waiting in the hall to greet her. It had been that evening, when the little scrap had cried unceasingly and none of them were able to soothe her that Sister Bertha had emerged from the shadows and taken Margaret in her arms. "Now then, young lady," she had announced, "this must stop – do you hear?" Margaret had stared at her in evident amazement, and, after a hiccup or two, had not uttered another sound. Sister Bertha had proceeded to rock the baby making curious clucking sounds and after a time she had called to the very young nun who had been assigned to look after the child; "Sister Alice, she is clearly hungry. Have you made up a feed for her? If so, fetch it at once." Ever since, of course, Bertha had been Margaret's devoted slave – and how the little monkey knew it!

Margaret's guardian, Sister Francis, with whom she spent her early years

An old lady sits in an armchair, thin grey hair caught in a bun. She is in a small room – sparsely, though adequately furnished – its institutional aspect saved by a low window-sill looking out on a garden ablaze with autumn colours. The door opens. Two nurses enter – one with a tray, which she places on a table beside the armchair – the other followed by a middle-aged woman. They remain in conversation near the door.

"As I say, Mrs Coulson – Mavis, isn't it? – she seems quite comfortable. How long is it since you saw her? Six months? Well, you'll notice a change, of course. She lights up a minute or so when a visitor comes and has a great deal to say. Sad we can't understand most of it. Living in the past, you know. First words are clear, then off she goes in a stream of nonsense! Maybe it will mean more to you? For instance, lately she has kept murmuring the words "Sister Frances" – sounds like a nun or something. Must be someone she knew long ago, I suppose? Gives us quite a turn sometimes. Seems to see her here." The nurse laughs apologetically.

"I hear them, but cannot answer – cut off from them in mist! Sister Frances, how can they know you were everything to me? Oh, many of the girls and staff at the Convent were frightened of you; and even I, Margaret. Yes, even I was a little in awe of you. But what security you gave me! A sense of being enfolded in your love and wisdom. I knew that behind all that severity lay deep affection – that I was somehow special to you. Sister Bertha loved me – and I think Sister Christabel too – but in a rather maudlin, old-maidish way. I suppose Sister Bertha actually idolised me. I only had to hug and tease her and she melted. Poor old thing! She ought to have married and had a family, instead of being a nun and maths teacher in a convent-school. The Convent! I can smell it now; see the fifth form class-room, and Sister Christabel's face when she saw what I had written on the blackboard before our Divinity lesson. What was it? 'There is no such thing as the Holy Ghost.' Oh yes, I was a rebel all right – and good at courting popularity with the other girls! Sister Christabel went purple, and I was sent straight to Sister Frances. For the first time I was frightened when she called me to her, and hesitated by the door. "Come here, Margaret," she called quietly, "sit on your usual stool beside me." I did so slowly, and she looked at me quizzically, nodding her head. "You know, Margaret, the Holy Ghost (or Spirit as I prefer to call Him) must be glad that you have begun to challenge His existence. It means of course that you have started your own personal search for Him!"

"Then there was that time on the netball pitch. We were waiting to begin our game. I was tying my shoelace when I heard two girls giggling close by. I looked up and caught

Rita's eye (I think that was her name?) She smirked and asked with artificial casualness: 'Margaret, is Sister Frances your real mother? Emily says (more giggles) that she is sure nuns shouldn't be married. But, well, we've never seen your mother at any of the school functions, and Sister Frances seems…well, you are her pet, aren't you?' She clapped her hand over her mouth, and I remember how I longed to hit her. Instead, I left the netball pitch and ran blindly towards the school buildings. I can see now the faces of the Governors as I charged into Big Hall, where they were finishing their ritual meeting. Sister Frances, who was seated at one end of the long table, gave one look at me and excused herself – telling young Sister Alice to wheel her to her room. "Now child," she said, as soon as we were alone: "Something has happened, I can see that. Try to be very calm, my dearest, and tell me about it". I leant against her knee, and I remember she put her hand on my shoulder. Choking with tears I told her, and for what seemed a long time afterwards she remained silent – automatically stroking my hair. At last she spoke: 'Long, long ago, when I was young, Margaret, your grandfather (yes, you had a grandfather, dearest) he and I were friends – part of a small group of young people who laughed and danced together". She paused, looking back over the years. "I had not yet joined our Order in those days. When I did so, of course, I said goodbye to all that – though I have always remained in touch with two or three friends from those old, other-world times. I wrote to your grandfather when his wife, your grandmother, died, and some years later I heard from him, begging me to help him. It appeared that…" (here she spoke the words very slowly) "…that his recently-married daughter and son-in-law had been killed…as a result of some accident abroad – a train accident, I believe." (I can see her calm, kindly old face quite clearly – looking oddly worried and preoccupied.) "I never knew the details. Their very young baby survived them, and was brought back to England by her nurse. My old friend – alone and widowed – felt quite unable to care for such an infant. He had become set in his ways – set and I think prematurely old. Having always retained a most exaggerated opinion of my merits, he wrote to me asking me to become your guardian and take charge of your education, in the event of his death. I think he may have had some premonition, as he died within a year of your coming to us." Her face brightened, "And so it was that you brought sunshine into our lives, Margaret! As for your old guardian, she has to admit that she is absurdly fond of you." I jumped up and threw my arms round her. She drew the hair from my tear-blotched face and kissed me. We stayed like that for a bit, and I felt the comforting warmth of her love.

"The mist is all round me. People come and go, but I am not in touch. There are voices, and someone is near me – bending over me. 'You know me, Margaret darling. It's

Mavis.' She gives me honeysuckle, and suddenly it is all there again...I see the house, smell the jasmine and honeysuckle creeping through the window. It was the first time I had encountered a real home. And then, there was Mrs. Beazley.

"I must have been five or six when I decided to become a nurse. I was quite firm about it, and everyone in the convent knew I was destined for St Thomas's. Some years later Sister Frances had raised the subject of my future with me. She told me she had been in touch with Miss Harcourt-Dunn, the Matron-in-chief. My name was entered for the autumn of 1925, when I would be 21. This would leave a gap of five years after I left school. Knowing my love for small children, she had put my name down for a well-known Nursery Nurses' College. I would thus be equipped to take a post as Nanny which would span the remaining gap.

After her guardian Sister Francis's death in the early 1920s, Margaret went to live with Mrs (Amy) Beazley, where she looked after Mavis and Freddy in the White House in Sussex

"I can see myself now in my new grey uniform, going to say goodbye to Sister Frances. I was excited – looking forward to escaping the boredom of the convent, which I had outgrown. At the same time, I hated leaving my guardian, and even that dear old fool Sister Bertha, who took my departure very badly. The next time I was in that room was when Sister Frances arranged for me to be interviewed by my employer-to-be. Mrs Beazley was about to produce her second child – the first being little more than a year old. Mr Beazley was half paralysed, and the arrival of two infants when Mrs Beazley was around the '40s mark presented challenges. I could see that she was nervous when she interviewed me – much more so in fact than I was. But instantly I felt drawn to her, and longed for the moment when I could join this family. I soon learned from Sister Frances that the feeling was reciprocal.

"Mavis is talking now – kneeling beside me. 'Mavis!' I open my mouth to tell her that having her there brings it all back – that I see quite clearly the small family group that day, the day I arrived at The White House to take up my first job. Mrs Beazley is holding Freddy on her knee. The toddler Mavis stands beside her, and I can see the mixture of jealousy and pride in her eyes, as she strokes the baby's head. 'Mavis!' A stream of strange noises comes out in place of all I want to say. Mavis is straining to understand me, and we are mutually locked in our frustration. Oh, I can see it in her eyes, while I – I… The mist is closing in again. I am in limbo."

Mavis looks in despair at the absent old woman in the chair. How can this – this travesty of humanity – be Margaret?

"The scent of honeysuckle laps round me. Slowly, my mind focuses. We are on the lawn below the old oak-tree. Mavis must be about five now. She is asking me for help with her cross-stitch picture, while Freddy (no longer a baby

Mr and Mrs Beazley (Edwin and Amy) having tea at the White House, Forest Row, in the 1920s

now but a wiry little four-year-old) pushes his Hornby train on a circular track. Mrs Beazley is seated reading, with absorption. She looks up, catches my eye: "Nanny, just listen to this. Isn't it wonderful?" She quotes from 'Pippa Passes', "how I hope that Mavis learns to love Browning as much as I do." The garden gate clicks, and Mr Beazley appears – moving slowly up the garden path. When I first arrived, he walked with one stick: now it is two. The children run to him, and greet him happily. "Wait," he says, and they draw back as Mrs Beazley brings up a canvas chair. He settles himself slowly, and Mavis jumps on to his knee, followed by Freddy, who snuggles up on the other side. Eileen, the little maid, sets up a table, and brings out tea. Sunlight filters through the oak branches, and I am aware of family happiness".

The huddled figure in the chair shifts. Mavis sees the shadow across her eyes – is conscious that she has lost her again. How can she re-kindle the faint spark? Her eye, travelling round the institutional room, in some desperation alights on the photograph of a nun. Sister Francis! How well she remembers it from old days. As a small girl she was always fascinated by the fine, aristocratic features – looking out on the world in wrinkled wisdom from her stiff white nun's coiffe. Nanny (Margaret) always had it by her bedside, in the night nursery. Mavis, who had been relegated to her own bedroom, used to slip in sometimes and gaze at the old face, sometimes talking to it gently. Now, she takes the worn photograph and kneeling again beside Margaret holds it in front of her. "Margaret, darling, how well I remember this…Margaret!", more loudly, "how you loved her, didn't you – your Guardian Frances?"

"I hear you, Mavis, through the veil. Why, though can I not communicate?" Love my guardian? She was mother, father, teacher and friend to me as I grew up. Love her! It was more like adoration… Oh, I see so clearly the moment when Mrs Beazley came to tell me that Sister Frances was dying and asking for me. The time had come for me to leave for St Thomas's. I was in the night nursery, packing. Mrs Beazley put her arm round me, explaining that my guardian only had a few hours to live…that she would drive me to St. Andrew's, that we must leave at once. From then on I never stopped shivering. I had never seen anyone die and now, the person I loved best was about to do so. I knew she was very old, but then she had been chair-bound and elderly all my young life. I had always taken it for granted. Mrs Beazley came with me to the bedroom door. She tapped, then left me, with a squeeze of the hand. I let myself in quietly. She looked very small in the heavy mahogany bed. Sister Christabel and Sister Bertha knelt beside her, and their eyes were red. For a time I stayed without moving, but she must have felt I was there. "Margaret!" It was only a whisper, but in a second I was at her side. The frail hands grasped mine, and her whole face lit up. "Margaret darling" – again the whisper, "you mustn't worry about the future." (Here a fit of coughing interrupted her.) "Mrs Beazley has told me… she…they all love you, darling, and…they will be a family for you." The whisper faded and I bent and kissed the wrinkled old face I loved so much. Then, she was gone. Sister Frances."

For a moment the crumpled figure in the chair bent its head, and Mavis was alarmed. What hidden memories had she unleashed with that faded photo of an old nun?

Mrs Beazley tried to catch me as I stumbled unseeingly from the room. I knew she was there, of course, but at that moment I wanted to punish everything and everyone I came in contact with and I pushed her aside.

Seeing her face a minute later in the dimly-lit convent passage, I knew I had successfully hurt her.

This time the figure in the chair slumped still further into a small heap. There is a tap on the door and an elderly nurse enters. Mavis rises quietly to her feet. "Nurse, I think she is asleep. I'll go now. I'm staying at the Crown, so shall be back tomorrow. I think I got through to her, but it's hard to tell." She leaves.

Margaret's Story – CHAPTER SIX

"Look what I've brought you, Margaret.'" Mavis is carrying a large package. The room – normally drab and institutional – is today glowing with autumn sunlight. Margaret's chair has been moved slightly – to face a garden she cannot see.

"I saw these in the antique shop in Sea Road … thought they'd be just right for you. She unpacks her parcel, and carefully places two Old Chelsea cups and saucers on the bed-tray beside the chair. "There! That will cheer things up a bit; and I know how you always loved old china." She stands back, surveying them with satisfaction. "Can you see them, darling? Aren't they pretty?"

"Mavis!" For a moment the distorted old face is radiant. "I…your mother …" And then once more it is gibberish. "The mist is rising between us, Mavis. Why, why can't I communicate with you – tell you that the tea-cups have brought it all back? It was my birthday, I think, and Mrs Beazley had come up from the country to see me at Thomas's. I had taken the day off, and met her at the door of the Nurses' Home. We went up to my room, and I helped her with the large package she was carrying. Perrot, the friend I shared with, was on duty, so we had the place to ourselves. We placed the parcel on a small table and I unwrapped it, Mrs Beazley watching my expression with amused affection. I had never before received such a magnificent present: a complete tea set, patterned in small roses! I made tea, I remember, from the old kettle out in the corridor. We sat and talked as we drank, and I told her something of my new life as a probationer. "How extraordinary to think that already you have been here six months, Margaret! Long enough, I'm sure, to have made a good many friends. Tell me about them: on your days off with us you spend most of the time with the children, and there never seems a moment to talk about your own life – though of course you have talked about Perrot, your Swiss friend." She watched me with obvious approval as I refilled our cups; and I thought how elegant she looked – her clothes not exactly smart, but in comfortable good taste. I was proud of her, and hoped people would see her with me when the time came for her to leave. "Oh yes," I answered casually, "of course I have friends: Latham, Norton, Grant… Haven't I mentioned them?" I did not add that all three of them vanished on their days off to what I imagined were something like stately homes…that some days previously I had overheard Deborah Grant remarking conversationally to Emily Norton. "Margaret Leigh is an odd fish… Haven't you noticed she doesn't seem to have any family to go to? Most of her days off are spent with a family where she was once Nanny.___ Imagine!" – she tittered. No, I didn't tell her that – nor that the new House Surgeon, Neil

Fenton, seemed to be unmistakably interested in me…that he used every opportunity in the ward to enlist my assistance with a patient…and that I – I who had never before had a boyfriend, was flattered and oddly comforted.

"I was due to spend my next day off, the following Wednesday, with the Beazleys. On the Monday evening there was a bit of a crisis. The fishmonger at the far end of the ward on the right had an epileptic fit. No warning, nothing whatever in his case-history. We couldn't bring him round. Sister called me urgently into her office. 'Fetch Dr Fenton at once, Nurse. He's on the next ward. Hurry.' I sped off, and met him coming out of Ward E. As he and I ran he turned towards me; "Are you free for dinner tomorrow night, Nurse? About 8.30ish?" I nodded, my heart leaping, then we were running down the ward, where the fishmonger's bed was already screened off. The man had swallowed his tongue, and over the next few minutes Neil Fenton wrestled to retrieve it. Someone called for a bedpan, and I was off to the other end of the ward. He passed me on the way out, and managed to whisper; 'The Blue Cockatoo, in Maunsel Street. I'll wait for you there."

"I went down to the country next morning and spent the day with Mrs Beazley and the children. It was Freddy's birthday and I had found him a clockwork spider. For Mavis there were dolls' spoons and forks, to compensate her for not being the centre of attention. Money was so tight for me that these purchases were the result of much searching and calculation; but it was worth it to receive their hugs of joy.

"He was seated at a table in the Blue Cockatoo, and rose as I came through the door. I had made some excuse to Mrs Beazley about needing to be back at the Hospital earlier than usual, feeling that I would wait till next time before telling her about Neil. She and Mr Beazley had given me a sea-green chiffon dress for Christmas, and I wore this – knowing that it suited my eyes. Neil appeared to think so, anyway, and my first 'dinner-date' passed like a dream. At the end of the evening he suggested that we walk home. It was moonlight, and the Thames, normally drab and filthy, looked like a silver ribbon as we crossed Westminster Bridge. 'We must do this again – soon," he said, almost tenderly and when he left me near the Nurses' Home he kissed me. "Ah, Neil! You little knew what that evening meant to me."

In fact, it was three weeks before we had another evening together. Unexpectedly I was put on temporary night-duty, and there was no opportunity for a chance meeting on the ward. However, the day after I re-joined Ward C, I saw him examining a new patient near the door. In due course I was able to find an excuse to go to the ward-kitchen, and we met in the passage outside. "Margaret! I've missed you… Yes, I know you were on night-duty, but…let's arrange to dine together again as soon as possible." We heard footsteps approaching, and he said hurriedly; "Meet me at the same place on Friday. Can you?" I nodded, and quickly turned away as Bentworth, the staff nurse, passed by. I thought she looked curiously at me.

We had hardly begun dinner that Friday night when Neil told me he wanted to take me down to Gloucestershire and introduce me to his family. "You and Susan, my sister, would like each other, I know you would," he said eagerly. "As for my father, he adores pretty ladies – particularly if they are good horsewomen. We can easily mount you, you know." He must have seen my expression, for he stopped suddenly. "Margaret, my dear, you do hunt, don't you? Somehow I took it for granted… Oh, what an ass I am! We all do it, you see – my family, all our friends… But, probably your people aren't interested… Imagine, darling," and he took my hand across the table, "I don't even know where your people live! Somehow – I don't know why – I thought your father might be an Army man. Am I right? Or perhaps a politician?" He gave me a smiling, affectionate look, which quickly changed to concern. "Margaret! You are quite white. And your eyes… Look! I'll pay the bill and we'll get out of here. Is it…can it be something I said?" And he rose quickly, calling for the waiter to bring the bill.

While he was paying, I sat as if stunned. It seemed suddenly very cold, and I pulled on my cardigan. So, once again the Enemy had struck. I had a clear vision of arriving at Neil's home. There'd be a butler, of course; and probably I'd be seated next to Neil's father at dinner. "Well, Miss Leigh, I think I can promise you a good day's hunting tomorrow… What, you don't ride. How…" he would cough suddenly. And later, when the ladies were alone, Neil's mother would ask; "My dear, are you related to Daisy, Leigh? We were at school together, you know… No? Well, do tell me a little about your family. Neil talked about you last time he was here…seemed to think your father was in the Army? What's that you say, my dear? You haven't any family? Brought up in a Convent, were you? Really, how sad!"

Neil tried to call a taxi, but I insisted on walking back across Westminster Bridge. The river was covered in mist, and I wept all the way. Neil walked with his arm round me, clearly mystified. At the door of the Home I pulled myself together. "It's no good, Neil." I swallowed. "I've never been near a horse, I have no parents, and the Mother Superior of a Convent brought me up! What's more, before coming to Thomas's, I was a children's Nanny!"

"She became rather excited after you left yesterday, Mrs. Coulson." Matron, sparse-haired and worn down by years of caring for the mindless, stops in the passage outside Margaret's door. "She was clearly re-living the past, you know. In fact, both Sister and I had the strong impression that those pretty tea-cups you brought her had somehow re-awakened a part of her mind." She smiles – a concerned, tired smile. "No doubt you think me fanciful, Mrs. Coulson, but I assure you this was the impression made on us. In any case, whatever it was, the experience quite tired her out; and she has slept from the time you left till a short time ago. In fact, I think Nurse has only just finished giving her her breakfast." She puts her hand on the door knob of Margaret's room and hesitates a little. "I'm sure you'll understand me, Mrs. Coulson, when I suggest it would be wiser to cut your visit to a minimum today. It seems such a pity when you've come such a distance, but … one feels all this must be quite a shock to the system." She turns the door knob: "Why, see who's here, my dear! Just looked in for a short time. Now, isn't that nice for you?"

"I've done her no good," thinks Mavis, eyeing the huddled figure in the chair with some despair. "Margaret, darling, I'm back again, as I said. Just for a quick visit, though, as John has to travel back to London. He has a very responsible job these days, you know…" Mavis' voice trails away as she thinks: "You poor love! As if it meant anything to you! Trouble is, one finds oneself talking compulsively in this room …" But there is movement in the chair. Margaret is leaning forward. "Mavis, you have…" And again that hideous torrent of gibberish.

"Mavis, why do I know Harley Street? I need to talk to you about it. Why are you the other side of this sea of mist? Harley Street! Yes, yes, it all begins to come back … I am in Miss Harcourt-Dunn's room. She is handing me something … of course. My birth certificate! I needed it because … because … I had to know. It was all building up. I was so different from everyone else in my 'set'. Louise had taken me home one weekend. She was always a quite ordinary girl to work with. Very plain really, with a fat face and thick arms and legs. Full of good nature, though. I had never thought about her much, but when she asked me I was pleased … very pleased, as invitations were rare. Her parents turned out to be big landowners, with an eighteenth century mansion somewhere – Hampshire I think. They treated me with benevolent condescension – rather as if I were a poor relation; and it was obvious that Louise had told them my history (or what was known of it).

"I never got over Neil, and thereafter held any potential successors at arms' length. Polly Ledbridge had a brother. He used to call for her occasionally when she had time off. He spotted me early on … made her ask me home to Kent one weekend. Ben was amusing to be with, and a terrific flirt. But, I made sure the affair went no further, knowing it would only end in humiliation.

"Soon after this episode I made a decision. I had to find out who I was, in order to be a valid person. The more I thought about it the more determined I became, and on my next day-off with the Beazleys, I questioned Mrs Beazley, feeling it was probable that Sister Frances had confided something to her before she died. I can see her in the garden at the White House. She was pruning roses and I was collecting up the discarded shoots, while Mavis and Freddy practised cartwheels. I felt very close to her as we worked. "Mrs Beazley" I tried to sound casual. "I know nothing at all about my family, you know. Sister Frances did tell me they had been killed in an accident. But who were they? It's…such a mystery." Mrs Beazley did not lift her head from the rosebush she was shaping. "I don't know, Margaret." She paused, then, "You really mustn't worry about this, Margaret. You are you, and that's all that matters. I only know what you know – what your guardian told me: that your parents both died tragically in a motor-accident. I am certain they were good, delightful people…" She went on to tell me how lucky I was to have been brought up by Sister Frances, and how she herself felt that I was now her unofficially adopted daughter… And she straightened herself and gave me a hug.

"Perrot was the only real friend I had at Thomas's. Marie came from Geneva, and apart from being very attractive in a buxom, hygienic sort of way, possessed a heart of gold and a developed sense of humour. She took me home with her one year. Her parents had a chalet near Gstaad, and we skied for a week there. Lord, what fun we had! It was all so new to me. I remember her father saying, "You are a terrible skier, ma petite" – (I had just run into him for the second time at the start of the ski-run) – "but you are, as you say in England, a big little sport." And he laughed till the tears came…"

Mavis glances at the figure in the armchair. A small smile is playing on the distorted old face. She gets to her feet quietly, and tiptoes from the room. The sight of that smile alone has made her complicated visit worthwhile.

136

"Yes, it was good to have Perrot as my room-mate. She was so sensible – well-balanced, I suppose you'd say. After I'd drawn a blank with Mrs Beazley about my family, I came back to London quite desperate. For one thing, I knew her so well that I felt sure she did have some knowledge. She had one of those faces incapable of hiding anything – which was why, I was certain she had kept her head down while I questioned her. I can remember flinging myself on my bed. Perrot, who was combing her hair at our tiny dressing table, threw an anxious glance at me. "Leigh," she exploded suddenly: "what is ze matter with you? You are not still worried about your family, are you? You English are so silly! As if a family mattered so much." Some time before – after the episode with Neil, I suppose – I had confided in her my background, or rather lack of it. Then, as now, she had listened to me in some wonder. Fiddling with her hair and staring almost fiercely into the mirror, she continued, "At least, Dieu merci, we have no lords and knights in Switzerland." Of course (this was half to herself) "we do have bankers." And she gave that absurd giggle of hers. Good old Perrot! I can hear it now. What a friend she was! And yet, somehow I had to spoil things – even with her – with my ridiculous touchiness. "H'm!," I snorted sarcastically, "all very well for you to talk. Bankers indeed! Everyone knows that your own father is a banker, and you are his darling." I glared at her, and saw her expression change. She went very red, and clenched her fists in an effort at self-control. There was silence for a moment, and when she spoke the words came out in gasps, "Leigh, do not you ever say such things to me again. If you do, I shall no more be your friend… Why do you have to… to defend yourself always – and with such cruelness?" She was crying now, and after a moment she left the room. For two days afterwards she wouldn't speak to me.

"Yes, good old Perrot! What a friend she was! She forgave me quickly, though I can't think why. Some weeks later, as we were returning from the theatre, (there were often free tickets for us nurses) she stopped in Trafalgar Square suddenly, "I have it, I have it, Leigh. Of course! Before I came from Geneva to Thomas's we had to send many papers… and yes, there was something to say I was the child of my parents – certificate of birth I think it was. You too must have had papers?" I shook my head. "Then your Sister Frances must have sent them to Miss Harcourt-Dunn without that you know. You were at work, perhaps? Don't you see, Leigh? On that piece of paper will be names – and this…this will say who is your Maman!" Perrot's English always deserted her at moments of excitement and I stared at her, my mind and pulse racing.

"I don't quite like the look of her, Matron." Nurse Stepson directs a puzzled gaze at the old woman in the chair. Matron crosses the room, and kneels beside Margaret. She feels her pulse, watching the wrinkled face. Then she straightens, "She's in a private world, Nurse," she observes wisely. "Look at that little smile. Almost as though she were going through some inner – well, rapture! I don't think we need worry too much – though I should keep a pretty constant eye on her at present. I'll be in my office if you need me."

"I waited at least a couple of minutes before I nerved myself to knock on Miss Harcourt-Dunn's door. She had the reputation amongst the young nurses of being some kind of magnificent ogre, and Perrot, whilst urging me on, had admitted the prospect of seeking her out in her den was a daunting one. "Come in!" The voice from inside was cool, authoritative. I opened the door. "Come in, come in, child! Don't stand there as if you'd seen a ghost! Now, what is it?" Her grey eyes appraised me with some surprise. It was not usual for junior nurses to pay calls on her. "Come nearer, Leigh:" (It was astonishing how she remembered the name of every nurse.) "I shan't eat you, you know." Her laugh was like a trumpet. "There! that's better" – as I moved towards her desk. It was now or never: "Miss Harcourt-Dunn, please may I have a look at my birth certificate?" The words came out in a rush. There was a long silence. The face of our matron-in-chief was inscrutable. Then, "Of course, child", she replied matter-of-factly. Rising to her feet, she went to an immense filing cabinet, and began rummaging in it. As she searched, she continued to talk. "This seems to me a good opportunity, Leigh, to tell you that I am satisfied, very satisfied with your work. Indeed, I will go as far as to say that you have the makings of an excellent nurse." She looked up from the card index in front of her, and added, "I knew your Guardian, child. It would have given her pleasure to see how well you are shaping." She eventually pulled out a file. There was kindness in the grey eyes as she handed me the piece of paper: "I think this is what you want, Leigh. Keep it today, if you like. But see that I have it back by to-night." And she turned away from me.

Perrot sat cross-legged on her bed, my birth certificate in her hand. I can see her now – a frown on her normally serene face, high-lit by bright spring sunlight. "Leigh, I do not understand. On my Genevois paper there is the name of my parents. And I suppose it is the same with you English: this must be normal. Only, here is only a man's name – Ian Barker, I think it is. And look!" – passing me the piece of paper – "There is something below it. Gy…gynacologist!" She spelt it out carefully. "Well! What do we do now?" Together we stared at the words; but I had already seen them, on the way back from Matron's office, and my mind was working fast. "Perrot! Don't you see? This must be the man who delivered me – brought me into the world! You are right. There is nothing else on the certificate; and this means…this means that I must find Dr Ian Barker now, quickly! twenty four years have gone by since he wrote this. He must be quite an old man now. Famous, too, I expect. Perrot, come with me to the telephone room, and we'll search the phone book!"

Margaret and Keith at their wedding
in Guildford, in the late 1940s

LAST LAP: BUDLEIGH SALTERTON

It is the end, or nearing the end,
Of the day. The August sea is sapphire – wedged between
The headlands. Alternating oxblood, chalky white,
These roll around the bay like horses' heads – their manes
All flying forest! Far below, the tide is on
The turn. Old Trafford's being enacted on the beach,
With Dad convinced he's Botham! "Run up Mike! He'll stump
You!" In the distance Belle is hunting shells. The sand
Is ribbed between her toes…

In the retirement home for Little Old Ladies
All is quiet. The residents – according to
Their strength and temperament – have sought the garden. Blanche
Is hunched in apathy beside the steps, while Jean
Moves competently down the border, 'dead-heading'.
Over the sumach-fronds the sea is winking. All
Is enmeshed in heat… And Margaret? Margaret is once
Again a little girl of seventy summers back…
All stripped, all innocent.

"I stood in Harley Street, on the steps of No. 21, waiting for someone to answer the bell. It had been difficult to fix an appointment, for Dr. Barker was clearly a very busy man. Eventually, I had had to ask Sister for half-a-day off, in part-return for extra night-duty I was about to do. The maid who opened the door showed me into a waiting-room. I picked up a magazine, trying to take things calmly; but concentration was impossible. At last the summons came. I followed the maid down a dark corridor. She knocked, and opened a door already ajar: "Miss Leigh, Doctor."

I found myself in a light room, with a large bay-window. Close to the window was a highly polished desk, with chair pushed back. A man stood with his back to me, gazing out of the window at a small garden below. He swung round as I entered and said politely, "Good afternoon, Miss Leigh. I…" he looked slightly puzzled, "I am not quite sure to what I owe the pleasure of this visit? We can find no mention in our files of a patient of your name… Perhaps I should have received a letter from your doctor which has gone astray? In any case, do sit down, Miss Leigh." He motioned me to a chair. "I am of course delighted to see you!" He was grey-haired, and stooped a little. A nose like a falcon's beak gave him an almost predatory look; and I should have probably lost my nerve had I not seen his eyes. They were rich brown, and I was aware of innate kindliness as they rested on me enquiringly. "Dr Barker" – the words came out in a rush – "you obviously don't realise it, but you have, of course, seen me before!" I stopped, stifled by nervousness. There was silence. Then, "My dear young lady, if I am wrong I stand of course corrected; and look forward to your explanation" He beamed at me suddenly, and the falcon beak seemed to vanish, "Dr. Barker, I… Naturally you would not recognise me. After all, twenty four years have passed since you brought me into the world!" Once again I discharged my words fiercely. I can see the look of mild astonishment on his face. "Really, Miss Leigh, you still have me there! As a matter of course, after receiving your request for an appointment, my secretary went through our files in search of your name. She found nothing, and I am bound to say that I – old man as I now am – rarely make a mistake where names are concerned." Once again he beamed encouragement at me. "My dear," he murmured, seeing my discomfiture, "suppose you tell me exactly what brought you to me!" And suddenly, I told him everything, or nearly everything – opening my bag and handing him the slip of paper on which I had carefully copied the details of my birth certificate. He stared at it a moment. Then, rising suddenly to his feet, he walked to the window and gazed out at the small garden beneath. After a time, and still with his back to me, he murmured, half to himself, "Is it possible? Can you be the child my wife and I so much wanted to adopt? We were, and are, childless, you see… It would have meant so much… It was your grandfather, of course, who put a stop to it! Told us that he had made all arrangements for you to be brought up by a Mother Superior, in a convent… When I protested, pointing out that I was not a poor man, and that a child of ours would be assured of a good home in all senses, he replied brusquely that everything was now organised and there could be no question of a change of plan. An obstinate man, your grandfather – one of the most obstinate that it has ever been my misfortune to meet." Dr Barker sighed and blew his nose. "Oh, I can remember the occasion as if it were yesterday – how upset we were…the utter frustration of it all." He turned and faced me. "I must think, my dear. In such circumstances I could not easily forget your grandfather – nor can I feel any loyalty to him. But his name… What was his name?" Again he turned and looked out of the window. Suddenly he swung back. "I have it, my dear. Of course! How stupid of me! I knew it had something warm about it! Wollen! That's it! Mr Wollen! And wait! I think I think he lived in Guildford. Yes, I'm sure of it!" He was triumphant. "Mind you, I did not attend your mother at home. Oh no! Her father had, I afterwards realised, hidden her in a Kent village." He stared at me a moment, then cried, "But of course, my dear. Of course! It was the village of Leigh: hence undoubtedly your name."

Margaret's Story – CHAPTER TEN

The ticket collector at Guildford station gave me clear directions how to get to Briar Road. It had been quite easy to find the address in the Surrey Telephone Directory. "Only ten minutes walk it is, Miss. You say the name of the house is The Sycamores? Can't say I know it; but Briar Road's a short one, and there's not many houses there. Big ones, they are, too. You're sure to find it!" Six weeks had gone by since that afternoon in Harley Street. I needed my monthly whole day off for this expedition, and an unexpected spell of night-duty had upset all my plans. Now, though, I knew I was about to find the answer to my personal riddle – that it lay literally round the corner – in the heart of middle-class, residential Dorking. Dr Barker's words as we said goodbye returned vividly to me. "If and when your search is successful, my dear, try not to be too hard on your mother! My memory of her is inevitably very vague, you understand. But she appeared to me at the time to be a gentle, frightened girl – entirely dominated by your grandfather. Try to remember, hard as it may be, that she may too have suffered." Yes, I can see and hear him now, as he took my hand at the door of his consulting-room, his eyes full of concern. "I would like you to know, my dear Miss Leigh, that my wife and I would be most grateful if you would keep in touch with us!"

'The Sycamores' was typical of its period: a large turreted Victorian house at the end of a short drive culminating in a gravelled circle. I vaguely noticed a magnificent lilac tree, covered in purple flower. Otherwise I felt quite numb – almost a spectator, to tell the truth, of what was happening. I remember there were six stone steps leading up to the mahogany front door. I rang the well-polished bell, and could hear it pealing crisply through the house. A little maid appeared. "Good afternoon, Miss! I'm afraid Miss Wollen isn't here at present." She looked at me curiously. "Have you an appointment, Miss?" I ignored the remark. "In that case I should like to see Mr Wollen, if he is at home." I announced, with last-ditch bravado. "Oh dear no, Miss. Mr Wollen died some years ago." (Again she threw me a curious look). There's no-one here, and Miss Wollen won't be back from the golf-course till three o'clock." I looked at my watch. It was 2 pm. "Then I'll wait," I said firmly – summoning the remnants of my courage. The girl hesitated, but eventually showed me into a large drawing-room, with unyielding Victorian armchairs.

An hour later, I rose from one of those heavy chairs at the sound of a door opening outside the room. I caught a glimpse of my anxious, enquiring face in the huge gilded mirror on the opposite wall. Suddenly, framed in the doorway which was reflected along side my face, I saw a face stunningly like my own, even wearing the self-same expression.

It is a moment frozen in time for me, seeing my face twice over in that one shocked instant.

I have often thought of what it must have been like for Muriel, when she arrived back light-heartedly that late spring day and was confronted by me – epitome of her guilty past! I could hear the maid telling her in the hall that she had a visitor. She came quickly into the drawing room, and as she did so, I turned round from facing the mirror and we gazed at each other. For my part I found myself looking at a fresh-faced, slim woman in her mid-forties. 'But we are ridiculously alike.' I thought in astonishment; and clearly she must have had the same impression, for she stopped dead. "I…" she murmured; totally confused. "Do I know you, Miss?" "You do," I answered – conscious of being in control of the situation, "I am Margaret – your daughter Margaret Leigh."

I cannot remember what happened after that – only that we both continued to face each other, in heightening emotion. In the end, oh, in the end we were in each other's arms – weeping and talking in incoherent spurts. And it was I who was comforting Muriel. The little old woman in the chair seems to dissolve. Sister, passing the open door, sees her slumped in a small heap, and runs for help. That evening the phone rings in the Coulsons' Hampshire home. "Mrs. Coulson, I am sorry to disturb you, but I thought you ought to know we are a little worried about Mrs Miller. After you left we kept a constant eye on her, of course, and Sister reported that she appeared to be slipping further and further into what I call her private world. Her lips moved from time to time, apparently, and that little smile we both noticed seemed to…well, flash in and out at times… In the end Sister found her quite collapsed in her chair, and called me at once. Mrs Miller, her old face was still set in a happy expression, though her pulse was very weak and I sent for Dr Black. He agrees that she has probably been somehow re-living her life. Says we should keep her absolutely quiet, and let her sleep as long as she wants. Yes, please ring to-morrow – though she may still be sleeping, of course."

Mavis decides she should go down and visit Margaret again.

"There you are, dear. A nice cup of tea and some buttered toast. Just what you need after that long sleep of yours. What did Sister say? Two days and a night? Well, you'll feel all the better for it, I expect… Now then…" The nurse settles her tray on the little table beside the chair. Margaret gives her a twisted smile and tries to communicate. The usual nonsense emerges, and she becomes silent. "Well, not very talkative today, are we dearie? As a rule you've a lot to say to Nurse Anthea, haven't you? In your own language of course…" She smiles indulgently.

Margaret huddles in the chair, opening her mouth like a small bird as the nurse feeds her. "Why does she have to treat me like a retarded child? Oh, she means well, of course… It's not her fault that I am separated from her by this fog. How weary, how very weary I am today." So many people, so many things have passed through my mind lately… The ingredients of my life, I suppose – though now I remember nothing.

The door of the room opens and a very young helper enters. "Lovely postcard's just arrived for you, Margaret. Shall I read it to you? Looks as if it's come from abroad. Yes, fancy. It's from Egypt." Tossing aside long blond hair, she chatters away and plumps down on the floor beside the chair: "So… What does it say? Anne and I are having a splendid cruise on the Nile. We often think of you, Margaret, and of your time in Egypt with the QAs. Too bad it had to be cut short! One could spend many happy years here! Love, Freddy."

Egypt! Freddy. Yes, I recall quite

The Nile near Cairo.

clearly how we talked of my posting to Egypt – the day he broke up from his prep-school. I had left St Thomas's, and was on embarkation-leave. I got a lift over to the Beazleys. They had recently moved to Parrock Wood, a largish turn-of-the-century house with fine views over Ashdown Forest. We were in the drawing-room, and Mrs Beazley (what years it took me to call her Amy!) was telling the children about my new-found cousin – a cousin all alone in the world – who had been delighted to discover an unknown relative. Freddy, who was standing close to me, darted a look at the new tennis-racquet leaning against my suitcase, "I bet she gave you that, didn't she?" he commented with appreciation: "Are you going to live with her, Nanny – I mean Margaret?" "No, young man, I am not," I replied – "but of course I shall see her when I get back from abroad – just as I shall be seeing all of you," I added, giving him a hug. He hugged me back, and I thought what a good-looking little fellow he was in his school grey flannels – his dark good looks crossed with mischief. "You see," I continued, "I am now in the British Army a QA (which means Queen Alexandra) nurse. "What's more, we are off to Egypt next week. Isn't it exciting?"

Nurse Anthea and Sue, the volunteer, exchange looks. Margaret is looking over and far beyond them, into another world. Sue takes the tray, and quietly they slip out of the room.

"Strange how I can almost smell the military hospital at Ras-el-Tin…hear the shouts of the Suffragi in the kitchen. Yes, and I can see us now: four excited QAs leaning over the deck railings as our troop-ship eased its way into the Alexandria dock. From a nearby mosque came the call of the muezzin, and the city ahead seemed to bristle with minarets. As we made our way down the gangway, the smells of the Near East rose to meet us – those strange, beckoning smells spiced with mystery which seem to open doors. Louise clutched my arm: "Can you believe it, Leigh? This is the Middle East. I feel we're in another world." The voyage, overcrowded as the ship had been with troops, had had its high points, and, as the only women on board, the four of us had had the time of our lives. Now, though it was over, and we were impatient for the next stage. We had known for some time that we were to be split up. Louise was destined for the military hospital in Mustapha, Alexandria, I was bound for another in Ras-el-Tin, and Jean and Paula (who had trained at Guys) were off to the much larger Citadel Hospital in Cairo.

Ah, but the mist around me is heavier now – heavier and laced with spices. Through it I can see the little hospital, perched above the seething dock-quarter of Ras-el-Tin. The sun is setting in blood and violet across the bay, and yes, I can distinctly hear the dusk-noises rising from the little streets all round us.

Also, I hear Dan's voice – clear and insistent. "Come on, Margaret! why can't you let yourself go a bit? After all, we're only young once, and so on… Dan had been on the ship, and I had seen a lot of him. He was attractive, I suppose, in an unexciting sort of way. Fair, with small, neat moustache. Medium height. Very confident. A Captain, no less, in the Rifles: At the time I remember thinking him a satisfactory dancing partner, and a probable asset when we reached Egypt.

Ralph, his brother officer, had been Louise's partner on board. The regiment was stationed in Alex, and after we had been there a couple of weeks, it was arranged that the men should pick us up at our respective hospitals and take us to dinner. Compared with London training hospitals, the rules existing in Egypt were undemanding. Both at Ras-el-Tin and Mustapha the establishments were small: a Sister-in-charge presided over three other Sisters.

Dan and Ralph had booked a table at a Greek taverna. I seem to remember the food was indifferent, but the music excellent. Louise was rather in love with Ralph, and the two sat talking endlessly, while Dan and I spent much time dancing. I was not used to wine, and felt exhilarated. Dan was a particularly good dancer, and as we two-stepped within the narrow confines of the dance-floor, he pressed me close. It was then that he made his suggestion. "Look Margaret! If you two girls can arrange your monthly day off together, Ralph and I will try to fix forty eight hours leave and we'll go to Cairo. How about that, now?" And he beamed at me, clasping me even closer. For a moment my heart leapt with excitement. Cairo: The Pyramids! sliding down the Nile in a felucca, perhaps…? And then, Cairo night-life, to complete the picture! Cairo night-life!" At that moment I began to consider the implications. It wasn't so much my convent upbringing that began to nag at me. (Indeed, you could have said that its restrictions made me all the more eager for adventures, to make up for lost time. No, it was something else) I weighed up my dancing partner, and decided that, agreeable and entertaining as he might be, there was something missing. He wasn't… wasn't, as Mrs Beazley would have said, 'quite out of the top drawer, Margaret.' And, no, I didn't want to get involved with him.

Curious how my whole attitude had changed since I had found Muriel. I no longer felt perpetually on the defensive. Instead, as Perrot had teasingly pointed out, shortly before we left Thomas's, "Leigh, what has come over you? You have suddenly become a real English SNOB. Only the aristocrats will do for you these days."

It was true, of course; and I pondered the effect on me of the discovery that my mother was a good bourgoise, and my soldier father something more.

Six months later, I did in fact go on short-leave to Cairo, but with someone very different from Dan.

The old head sinks; and once again Margaret's frail little body seems to shrivel… She sleeps deeply, in her chair.

Margaret's Story – CHAPTER ELEVEN

"Margaret! That postcard you had the other day from Egypt. My Dad was ever so interested. He was there, you see – ages ago, in the war. Lent me some pictures to show you. Only you've been sleeping most of the time the last few days, and Anthea said not to disturb you." Sue squats beside the chair. "Look Margaret, there's my Dad in his RAF uniform. Handsome, isn't he? Oh", (with a giggle), "there he is with his mates beside one of the Pyramids. He says the Nile is smashing … What are those boats called? Fe- fe- …?" To her surprise, a quiet voice from the chair completes the word: "Felucca:" "Why, Margaret, aren't you clever? Of course, though. You must have lots of memories, just like him. Did you ever go in a felucca?" Sue looks up at her eagerly. Margaret is staring ahead unseeingly, oblivious of the girl at her feet. Sixty years have fallen away. She is drifting down the Nile, with Colin at her side – a vast sail ballooning overhead.

"It must have been two or three months after our arrival, I suppose. Sister Murphy, the Sister-in-charge, told me to report for night-duty at the Isolation Ward at Mustapha, Louise's hospital. Only a temporary transfer; she assured me. A staff-nurse had gone sick with typhoid, and was likely to be invalided home. Just a case of holding the fort for a week or two. After that a replacement would arrive from the Citadel Hospital in Cairo. I remember I had mixed feelings. Ras-el-Tin was beginning to feel like home. I liked the easy, friendly atmosphere, and Sister Murphy's quiet efficiency. At the same time, it would be fun to be with Louise – who by chance was about to go on night-duty herself, on another ward. That evening Sister Fielding took me round the Isolation Ward and introduced me to the half-a-dozen patients there. She explained that all but one were recovering from typhoid. Corporal Maitland in the small room at the end of the ward was desperately ill with TB and might not last the night. I knew, of course, the drill for careful sterilisation and protective clothing, having done a short spell in Thomas's Isolation Ward. All the same, when I settled down at Sister's desk, I remember refreshing my memory on immunisation instructions before studying the previous day's log-book. Soon, the ward was quiet. During the long hours that followed, there was little disturbance – though I kept a close watch on Corporal Maitland. I was sitting reading, endeavouring, with a cup of tea, to while away the hours when I heard him; "Nurse! Nurse, I feel terrible."

I looked at my watch. It was 4.30 a.m. He couldn't have been more than twenty one; but the disease had transformed Corporal Maitland (oh, I remember that name!) into a wasted old man. I felt his pulse. He coughed wretchedly, and clung to my hand. "Don't leave me, Nurse. I… I want you to send a message to my girl, Mandy, and to my mum. Tell them…" He was haemorrhaging. I held his hand tightly, and through the ward window beside him could see the Egyptian dawn beginning to creep across Ras-el-Tin. There was a balcony leading off the ward, close to his bed. On an impulse I said, "Dawn is breaking outside, Bill. I'm going to lift you up in my arms so that you can see it." He weighed almost nothing, and it was easy to carry him through the door. For a moment we were cradled in rose and aquamarine, and somewhere down in the little streets below came the call to prayer. The tortured look on Bill's face faded. "Nurse," he whispered, "it's all right now… Everything's all right… So peaceful, it is! Tell them…" And suddenly he was gone. With difficulty I carried the limp body back to the bed, after which I went to summon the orderly.

By the time we went off duty at 8 am, he and I had laid out Corporal Maitland; I had also made my report to Sister Fielding.

He was buried in the Military Cemetery. Although I had only known him a few hours, I went to the funeral – as I liked to do when one of my patients died. Sister Fielding was with me, and as we were about to leave, a young subaltern approached us. "Sister, how good of you both to come along." I'd like to introduce myself – Lt Langdale (Colin Langdale). Corporal Maitland was one of my chaps, you know. What a tragedy this is: he put up such a gallant fight, too – against hopeless odds. You and I have met more than once, Sister – when I came to enquire about him. I don't think I have had the pleasure of knowing Nurse…?" His voice was a question-mark. Sister Fielding, who remembered him well, introduced me. He said quickly: "Sister, I want to thank you and all your staff for the splendid way in which you fought to save Bill Maitland's life. Sergeant Bull is also one of my men, and I have received a note from him telling me how wonderful you were, Nurse Leigh, the night the poor chap died. Bull's bed is at the end of the ward, you see, and he writes that he woke just before dawn to hear Maitland calling for you. Said he saw you through the glass partition, that you took him in your arms and held him by the window to see the dawn. Nurse Leigh, we are very grateful to you." He cleared his throat, and I saw the look on Sister Fielding's face. I had omitted that detail in my report.

Colin Langdale walked with us to our cab. As Sister Fielding stepped in, he asked me in a quick aside whether and when he could see me again. Yes, that was how it all began. At that moment I fell deliciously in love with Colin – and he, perhaps, with me.

"Look, Nurse Anthea! Look at her face! Just like a young girl's, isn't it? Not really, of course – but somehow you don't seem to notice the wrinkles now… See! She's smiling. Wonder what lovely dreams she's having?" Sue winks at Nurse Anthea beside her, and pulls up Margaret's rug, giving her a motherly pat on the shoulder. To her surprise

Margaret, who has been sleeping solidly for the last couple of days, stirs and opens her eyes. Sue quickly picks up the Egyptian card, holding it close to her. She is rewarded with a misty smile of pleasure.

That could have been our felucca. Only it was early evening when we walked down the quay-side at Luxor and Colin hailed the boatman. As we clambered in the sun was sliding down the horizon, to the left of the Valley of the Kings. All was crimson and gold – with a faint glow over the Royal Tombs. At first there was no wind. The boat crept almost imperceptibly towards the other shore. Suddenly, though, the huge sail filled, and we were off… gliding effortlessly over the darkening Nile. We sat in the bows, and Colin reached for my hand.

It had all the elements of a dream. As crimson became purple and gold merged into aquamarine, we floated lightly, silently, beside the far shore. I can see and hear flashes from that ancient world; a woman returning late from the well, her amphora held proudly on her head; the outraged bray of a donkey and a man's shout in the darkness; two young boys on a raft quite close to us, beating the water with paddles to make the fish leap into their net. Earlier in the day, we had admired the same scene in a tomb-fresco. The sense of timelessness was all around us.

We had dinner in a small restaurant close to Karnac. "You have beautiful eyes, Margaret," he murmured: "greenish grey eyes – like water in a forest pool." That pleased me, and I let him stroke my hair, gently, feeling its silkiness. "Tell me about your boy-friend in England, darling. I'm sure he's not worthy of you! I wonder if he is a doctor … or perhaps a soldier." His voice was teasing. "Come on, Margaret: And when you've finished, it'll be my turn." I was troubled. "What makes you think I have one?" I replied quickly. "As a matter of fact, there's no-one, at the moment! Colin laughed, "Don't tell me a warm, lovely girl like you hasn't got a young man. I simply don't believe it!" And then…then he told me about Laura. They were unofficially engaged, and would probably announce it when he went home on leave next month. She was a gorgeous brunette apparently much involved in 'Health and Beauty' – Prunella Stack and all that. He knew she was having a good time while he was away…but why not? After all, (with a mischievous smile at me) he himself was lucky enough to have found a charmer to spend his off-duty with! I listened, unbelievingly. This, from someone I had imagined to be as much in love as I was. It wasn't…couldn't be true. Surely he was pulling my leg – though if so the joke was a very sour one.

We walked back to the hotel, and though I felt dead inside, I let him put his arm round me. It was our second night in Luxor, and we had broken the journey in Cairo en route. On each occasion, Colin had behaved with exemplary correctness. Two single rooms had been booked, and I was 'my cousin Miss Leigh' to the desk-staff. Tonight, however, he showed no disposition to leave me at my door, apparently quite unaware of my feelings. There was a tussle in which he called me a prudish little nun, but I managed to free myself, and somehow succeeded in slamming and bolting my door. Poor Colin. What a mixture he was: good-looking in a slim, dark confident way: Charming as a companion, too – when his considerable knowledge of Egyptian history made him the perfect guide… in the Royal Tombs, or at the Temple of Luxor, for example. Thoughtful for others at times (and even compassionate, where Corporal Maitland was concerned). And yet? And yet, serenely sure of his own philosophy of living, and of his own ability to fit others into it! Next morning, we made our way back to Alexandria – changing trains in Cairo. As it turned out, I never saw him again.

But now Mavis realises that Margaret's mind is running like a tickertape –sometimes in short bursts, sometimes in a strange tranquillity…

We are back in Alexandria and again I am on duty in Ras-el-Tin Hospital. The tickertape in my mind runs fast now, and I am beginning to cough – that tell-tale cough…Yes! Sister Fielding is almost constantly with me now. Ironic – isn't it? – that I am here to nurse patients and now it is Ward Sister Fielding who is nursing me. The tickertape shoots by, images are half hidden in this stifling mist and Sister Fielding is nursing me devotedly.

No one is allowed near me, and I think I know that I am critically ill with T.B. In and out, in and out. This all-embracing fog on top of it all makes it impossible… How I long for Sister Frances, and the cool of Mrs Beazley's garden. For some reason nothing seems to matter and there is no fear… Suddenly the fog lifts! Sister Fielding tears in. Her eyes tell me that I have turned the corner – that soon I will be sufficiently recovered to be invalided home. That same day Sister Fielding told me that I was out of danger, there arrived a letter from Muriel telling me that she was making a small bedsitting room for me at the large house in Dorking. I could hardly wait! After that I remember nothing – only that Muriel, my re-found mother, is on the quayside to meet me as we dock at Southampton. She sweeps me off to that large middleclass house in Dorking. It is here that I slowly recuperate. To anyone who wants to know more, the legend of the long lost cousin is developed.

Mavis recalls how she sensed the relationship between Margaret and Muriel continue to deepen. She reflected how lucky it must have been that Margaret's grandfather's affluence had been able to cover their winter trips abroad. Margaret knew the doctor would categorically refuse to allow her to winter in England. Wherever they went – Madeira, Majorca, or Hyères – Muriel opened her season (so to speak) at their hotel with a personal dinner to which she would invite carefully chosen guests. Mavis suppressed a smile. Dear old Muriel – she was so determined to find a 'young man' for Margaret, and in their last pre-war dinner, she succeeded. Muriel felt so at home with him. He was much nearer her age, of course, and there was no self consciousness. But always Margaret herself felt safe with him – so at one with him.

The hunched figure in the armchair began to move excitedly. Oh, she can see him, as he shyly introduces himself: a timid Scot from Aberdeen, on his way home to take early retirement from his firm in Calcutta. He was nearly twenty years older than her but tongue-tied as they both were at first, and heaven knows how long it took him to nerve himself to propose marriage, Margaret knew that this was 'it'.

The 'flashbacks' are becoming increasingly blurred…

Margaret is suddenly radiant. She attempts to move up out of her chair, stretches out her hands and then collapses totally. The journey back in time is over. This time her sleep is permanent.

Mavis Coulson, Selborne - 2005